...*The Mole of Vatican Council II* is sold as historical fiction but reads more like a history book in many chapters, which, incidentally, is a strength in this case. It details at length desperate efforts by Curial traditionalists to sabotage the Second Vatican Council (1962-1965) to "save the faith" — and how close they came to achieving that objective.

The heart of the novel, however, traces those traditionalists' frantic attempts to unmask and silence a priest who, under the pseudonym of Xavier Rynne, wrote a series of eye-popping articles for *The New Yorker* spilling the beans on backroom dealings and attempted subversion of the goals Pope John XXIII and his successor, Pope Paul VI, had for the council.

Fr. Francis Xavier Murphy was an American Redemptorist priest serving as a theological adviser to a Redemptorist bishop during Vatican II. This allowed him access to all sessions, as well to the hallways and elevators where he learned of efforts by Cardinal Alfredo Ottaviani and other conservative prelates to undermine the council. The novel details how Murphy became Xavier Rynne, how his articles became must-reads for lay Catholics and clerics alike and how he became the target of Ottaviani and others' rage.

Despite the author's insistence in the book's foreword that *The Mole* "should be read as historical fiction," both the foreword and epilogue let readers know that most of it is based on primary source documents: Murphy's articles, diaries, personal letters, interviews with Columbia University's Oral History Research project and even files secretly kept on Murphy and given to Zmuda by anonymous sources. The primary sourcing makes the book more interesting than it might otherwise be, but also more frightening; readers get a close-up view of how important — and precarious — that time in church history was….

The Mole of Vatican Council II is an entertaining and illuminating read overall, but readers should go into it knowing it won't read like most traditional historical fiction. It is for Catholics who like inside-baseball analysis, for non-Catholics who crave the "fly on the wall" experience of an institution that still holds sway in the world and, dare I say, for every person who never wants to go back to where we've been.

Review published August 31, 2024, and written by Renée Schafer Horton. See full review at *National Catholic Reporter* online (ncronline.org).

THE
MOLE OF
VATICAN
COUNCIL II

"To think of a mole as that which digs underground misunderstands the meaning of the mole as a spy. A spy's task is not to hide himself where no one can see him, since he will not be able to see anything himself. A spy's task is to hide where everyone can see him and where he can see everything."

Viet Thanh Nguyen, *The Sympathizer*

THE MOLE
OF VATICAN
COUNCIL II

THE TRUE STORY OF
"XAVIER RYNNE"

RICHARD A. ZMUDA

THE MOLE OF VATICAN COUNCIL II
The True Story of "Xavier Rynne"
Richard A. Zmuda

Edited by Gregory F. Augustine Pierce
Cover and text design and typesetting by Andrea Reider

Published by ACTA Publications, 7135 W. Keeney Street
Niles, IL 60714 (800)397-2282 www.actapublications.com

Paperback ISBN: 978-0-87946-732-6
Hardcover ISBN: 978-0-87946-733-3

Library of Congress Number: 2024933036

Printed in the United States of America by Total Printing Systems

Year 30 29 28 27 26 25 24

Printing 10 9 8 7 6 5 4 3 2

Text printed on 30% post-consumer recycled paper

To

Fr. Francis X. Murphy, C.Ss.R.
aka Xavier Rynne

As promised.

CONTENTS

Introduction   1

Chapter I: *"Habemus papam!* – We have a pope!"   3

Chapter II: "A Council!"   37

Chapter III: "A brilliant gambit"   63

Chapter IV: "The smallest of windows can shed
                light on the greatest of truths."   93

Chapter V: "Prophets of Doom"   123

Chapter VI: "Who the hell is Xavier Rynne?!"   155

Chapter VII: "It is the *Pauline* Council now!"   181

Chapter VIII: "We will change everything back
                to the way it was!"   209

Chapter IX: *"Magno cum dolore* – With great pain"   229

Chapter X: *"Ite in pace* – Go in peace."   261

Epilogue   291

About the Author   295

Acknowledgments   297

Appendix: Ecumenical Councils of the
                Roman Catholic Church   299

For security purposes, the passport on the front cover was issued exclusively to cardinals and bishops attending Vatican Council II (1962-1965).

It featured the gold-embossed Coat of Arms of Pope John XXIII.

Introduction

The primary source used in the writing of this book was *Vatican Council II* by Xavier Rynne (Father Francis Xavier Murphy), published by Orbis Books in 1999, which included his series of articles published in *The New Yorker* from 1962-1965. Rynne's unrivaled eyewitness descriptions of the Council's deliberations are incorporated herein at the personal request and with the permission of Father Murphy himself.

It was in 1996 that I received a call from Father Murphy, a priest in my Annapolis parish, who knew that I was a teacher of literature and a freelance writer. He was in his early eighties at the time and weak from a prolonged illness. He asked me to ghost-write a new introduction to an anniversary edition of his book on Vatican Council II. I readily agreed.

While working on that project, I realized that by editing out much of the extreme theological detail in that book there could be a riveting storyline that would be of interest to not only multiple generations of Roman Catholics around the world but also to a much broader religious and non-sectarian readership. In his writings, Xavier Rynne (Father Murphy) single-handedly brought to light the subversive efforts of certain powerful conservative cardinals, virtually all members of the Roman Curia, that almost brought Vatican Council II to an ignominious end. It was a story that simply had to be told.

Father Murphy gave me unlimited access to his extensive archive of writings and personal correspondence, some of it likely long forgotten, even by him. I supplemented this with transcripts from his interviews with Columbia University's Oral History Project and from files secretly kept on Father Murphy, unbeknownst to him, in both Rome (where I traveled twice to research this book) and the United States.

This book should be considered historical fiction. While all of the Church hierarchy, dates, issues, and decisions are properly identified, private conversations between the various protagonists, as well as the composite characters of Cristina and Luciana, have been invented by me but are considered essential to the authenticity of the overall storyline.

With heartfelt gratitude to Father Murphy, with whom I developed a close working relationship during the latter years of his life, I hope this book brings to light one important aspect of his remarkable legacy.

Richard A. Zmuda
Annapolis, Maryland
February 2024

CHAPTER I

"Habemus papam! –
We have a pope!"

The slightest wisp of milky white smoke floated lithely upward, dissipating quickly amidst the gentle evening breeze above St. Peter's Square in Rome. In an instant, the boisterous conversations and prayerful invocations of two hundred thousand faithful suddenly receded into a reverential, anticipatory awe.

It was the evening of October 26, 1958, Day Two of the papal conclave to elect a successor to Pope Pius XII. All eyes gazed longingly toward the cap atop the simple metal chimney pipe running up alongside the unadorned masonry façade of the Sistine Chapel, to the right of St. Peter's Basilica.

Earlier that day, during the morning session of the secretive gathering of cardinals, as well as on the preceding first day of the conclave, dense clouds of black smoke had been emitted skyward, signaling that a pope had not yet been chosen. However, now, after a third round of balloting, a new, smallish plume bellowed and the coloring was unmistakably white, offset dramatically against the darkening early evening sky. There was collective, escalating excitement, hugs were effusive, prayers of ecstatic joy proclaimed. A Vatican radio announcer gleefully declared "*È eletto un papa!* – A pope has been elected!" For close to five minutes there was jubilant bedlam, but then some in the crowd began to notice a subtle darkening of the plume, initially light gray then slowly but decidedly black. Hushed whispers quickly disbursed throughout the multitude. Then suddenly, no more smoke. Silence. Disbelief. Confusion. A new pope had apparently not been chosen after all.

Two stories below that confounding emission, chaos reigned within the increasingly claustrophobic confines of the Sistine Chapel. Under the imposing scrutiny of Michelangelo's magnificent fresco *The Last Judgment*, fifty cardinal-electors, who were gathered in the exact same location where their predecessors had similarly deliberated since the 1400s, were locked in a political tug-of-war that most of them feared could have revolutionary, if not mortal, implications for the future of the Catholic Church.

———◆———

On the previous morning of October 25th, the very first day of the conclave, fifty venerable chairs had been aligned along the lateral walls of the Sistine Chapel, abutting the Raphael tapestries depicting the lives of Saints Peter and Paul. Each chair had an identical canopy attached above it, a symbolic sign of equal dignity among the cardinal-electors. As soon as a new pope was chosen, he would ascend to the altar, sit upon the papal throne underneath its own singularly magnificent canopy, and offer the chosen name for his pontificate. In response, the other cardinals would tug on a rope attached to their respective seats to lower their canopies in deference to the new pontiff. One by one, they would then approach the altar, genuflect and pledge their fealty.

As the College of Cardinals made their way into the Sistine Chapel for the opening of this conclave, their sober demeanors betrayed the historic gravity of the moment. The passing of Pope Pius XII had not been unexpected; in fact, his 19-year papacy had been one of striking longevity for the modern era. However, his death on October 9th had come on the cusp of rising social and political unrest that would soon erupt into the contentious 1960's – a rebellious, revolutionary, societal movement that had been quietly fomenting for years, and which had implications far more global than the much-publicized demonstrations in the United States. This the gathered cardinals implicitly knew, and they feared the Roman Catholic Church itself was not immune to similar upheaval.

The near dozen cardinals from the powerful Curia, or Vatican cabinet, as well as an uncertain plurality of the other cardinal-electors in attendance at the conclave, were staunch traditionalists, conservative to their very core, firmly believing that the Church should act as an immovable anchor against radical tides of change. Yet an undetermined number of the other assembled cardinals felt just as strongly that the Church should modernize and adapt itself to the changing world around them. There was no middle ground.

The unequivocal leader of the ultra-conservative bloc was Alfredo Cardinal Ottaviani, age sixty-seven, head of the oldest and most powerful of the Curia departments, the Congregation of the Holy Office, known for prior centuries as the Sacred Congregation of the Universal Inquisition. He felt quite at home.

Ottaviani was born the second-to-last of twelve children of a Roman baker in the shadows of St. Peter's Basilica. In effect, he had been the ultimate Vatican insider since his birth. He was easily the most recognized and outspoken conservative voice among the gathered cardinals. In fact, the Latin motto of his cardinalatial Coat of Arms was "*Semper Idem* – Always the Same." He literally wore his heart on his vestments.

Ottaviani was a tall, powerfully-built, intimidating figure. He was tight lipped, in a smug, arrogant way, giving the impression that he knew everything and would aggressively argue with anyone who held a contrarian view. And yet at times he seemed to convey an easygoing affability, especially with first-time introductions. But those who knew him well understood that this was simply a ploy to surreptitiously assess potential adversaries in a non-confrontational way, to initially disarm them. Conversation came easy to Ottaviani, but he soon grew impatient with small talk if it was not a means to an eventual end, especially one that he concurred with. His innate inclination was serious, focused; however, when his passion was piqued, often around political and global issues that butted up against his conservative worldview, he roared with fervency. His bushy eyebrows overlay lids that did not let his eyes fully open, a subtle indication of his weakening vision. The resulting glare could be piercing. His fleshy neck offset an otherwise strong countenance; ironically, his small mouth did not seem predisposed to such a commanding voice. He was overwhelmingly self-assured, uncompromising, and feared. Because of all these traits, or maybe in spite of them, Ottaviani was grudgingly respected by colleagues and detractors alike. He was also intensely hated by a select but powerful few, in actuality more than he would ever anticipate. That would prove to be his undoing.

On that crisp afternoon of Saturday, October 25, 1958, Day One of the conclave to elect the new pope, Ottaviani entered the Sistine Chapel close behind the Dean of the College of Cardinals, Eugene Tisserant of France. Ottaviani walked with a confident swagger that was pretentious even by his own standards. Since more than a third of the cardinal-electors were Italian-born, Ottaviani felt certain they could keep the papacy well within their insular grasp that had served, at least in his mind, the Church so effectively for over 400 continuous years since the death of Pope Adrian VI of the Netherlands in 1523. In addition, Ottaviani and many of his fellow cardinals had been hand-picked by Pius XII, a similarly unabashed traditionalist. Ottaviani therefore believed that their allegiance to the status quo, to religious orthodoxy, and to the conservative ideals that he so passionately espoused was firmly on his side, or at least malleable to his intimidation.

In the days leading up to this conclave, Ottaviani himself was oft-mentioned as "*papabili* – papal potential." But he dismissed these notions, ironically coming off as humble in the process. He knew he was far too polarizing to sit on the Throne of St. Peter; he was much more comfortable operating within the powerful, covert framework of the Vatican Curia. But he did have in mind another candidate, an early favorite going into the conclave, Italian Giuseppe Cardinal Siri, the sitting Archbishop of Genoa. Cardinal Siri was the youngest of the gathered prelates, only fifty-two, but clearly a rising star within their ecclesiastic ranks. He was also resolutely conservative, but in a less confrontational way than Ottaviani. The endgame for Ottaviani was that by throwing his formidable support toward a successful election of Siri to the papacy, he would not only ensure an ongoing conservative powerhold in the Church for what could be one of the longest papal reigns in history but also virtually guarantee his own continued leadership of the Congregation of the Holy Office.

Giuseppe Siri was born in Genoa in 1906 and early on was recognized as a prodigy by his family. He had a vigorous, insightful curiosity, evident even as a young boy, coupled with a wonderfully engaging personality. He was also headstrong and stubborn, as many children can be, but much more aggressively so. His enrollment into the minor seminary in Genoa at age ten was as much an effort by his parents to nurture his intellectual gifts as it was to reign in his inherent recalcitrance.

Throughout his seminary years, Siri excelled academically and was soon a favorite of the staunchly doctrinal faculty. He was pegged as ambitious and politically astute, both qualities that would manifest dramatically in the coming years. After taking his final vow of ordination into the priesthood in 1928, he continued his studies at the Pontifical Gregorian University in Rome, earning a doctorate in Theology *summa cum laude*. Soon thereafter, at the age of only thirty-eight, he was appointed by Pope Pius XII as Auxiliary Bishop of Genoa, a remarkably fast progression within the Church hierarchy. Then, in 1953, at age forty-seven, he was elevated by Pius to the rank of cardinal, by far the youngest of his peers to be so anointed.

Siri's trademark horn-rimmed glasses, set atop a beak-like nose, gave him an air of prep-school superiority. He could be stern to the extreme and quick to anger, especially when provoked with viewpoints he deemed

carelessly unfounded or that ran counter to his own firmly
entrenched conservative perspectives. But he also retained
a youthful charm that endeared him to many, even those
who were pained by his unyielding traditionalism. His
keen intellect, political savvy and – most importantly –
staunchly orthodox views on Catholic teachings made
him the early frontrunner to succeed Pius XII and the clear
choice of Cardinal Ottaviani.

A papal conclave traditionally commenced on the
fifteenth day after the death of a pope. As the fifty cardinal-electors thus gathered in Rome in October 1958 for
the funeral of Pius XII, they were individually welcomed
by Cardinal Tisserant, who firmly cautioned each one that
canon law obliged them to "abstain from any form of pact,
agreement, promise or other commitment of any kind
which could oblige them to give or deny their vote to a
person or persons." That same statute, however, permitted
"the exchange of views concerning the election." Needless
to say, such generous and somewhat contradictory admo-
nitions offered significant room for political maneuvering
in the days leading up to the conclave, something Cardinal
Ottaviani was determined to exploit.

Ottaviani knew intimately well his long-serving counterparts within the Vatican Curia, whose ultra-conservative leanings he had duly cultivated and supported for
decades; he was certain they would follow his lead in the

upcoming balloting. For the non-Curial, but Italian-born cardinals, he was similarly confident that he could count on a solid majority of their support, especially with their fellow Italian Cardinal Siri as the front-running candidate.

As for the dozen or so cardinals from other countries, Ottaviani had never bothered to make more than a superficial effort toward their acquaintance over the years. He never felt that he had to. The Curia in Rome ruled with an iron, unyielding global fist on all Church-related matters, eschewing any outside dialogue that ran counter to their myopic worldview. Nonetheless, Ottaviani now went out of his way to play the role of informal concierge once these cardinals arrived in Rome. Since there had not been a papal funeral or subsequent conclave in close to two decades, he generously proffered advice and guidance on how to navigate the ancient formalities of the upcoming rites. Ottaviani's entreaties as an elder statesman and host were genuinely welcomed by the foreign cardinals. However, while these overtures seemed innocuous to the newcomers, for Ottaviani they were subtle opportunities to gauge initial leanings regarding the papal succession. And Ottaviani was heartened by what he heard.

The funeral of Pope Pius XII was an extraordinary public spectacle, with tens of thousands of Romans lining the streets along the procession route to pay homage to "their pope," who had been born in Rome and was now being laid to rest in his native city. His body then lay in state in St. Peter's Basilica on a bier surrounded by four Swiss Guards. One by one the cardinal-electors paid their prayerful respects, followed by a lengthy procession of the faithful. Then Pius was buried in a simple coffin in the grotto beneath the nave.

—◆—

At precisely 3:00 in the afternoon of October 25, 1958, all of the cardinal-electors gathered in the Pauline Chapel of the Apostolic Palace before moving to the Sistine Chapel for the opening of the conclave. Cardinal Ottaviani spied Cardinal Siri out of the corner of his eye. They briefly locked glances – penetrating, affirming – then quickly looked away. The stage had been set.

As the cardinals processed into the Sistine Chapel, they shuttled reverently to their respective chairs, the crimson of their mitres and vestments contrasting dramatically with the rich blues and vibrant hues of Michelangelo's surrounding frescoes. Once settled, Cardinal Tisserant read in Latin the ancient oath for a papal conclave:

> "We, the cardinal-electors present in this election
> of the Supreme Pontiff, promise, pledge and swear,
> as individuals and as a group, that whichever of us
> by divine disposition is elected Roman Pontiff will
> commit himself faithfully to carrying out the *munus
> Petrinum* of Pastor of the Universal Church and will
> not fail to affirm and defend strenuously the spiritual
> and temporal rights and the liberty of the Holy See."

At these words, more than a few of the cardinals peered subtly toward Cardinal Siri who, aware that others were watching him, bowed for an exaggerated, lingering moment. He then quietly exhaled, slowly raised his head and looked toward the altar, avoiding their inquisitive glances as Cardinal Tisserant began providing instructions for the voting.

The rite for a papal conclave had remained virtually unchanged for more than a thousand years. On the first day of a conclave, only one ballot was permitted. If no one received a two-thirds majority of the ballots cast, the cardinals would then recess to their temporary apartments adjoining the Sistine Chapel and reconvene the next morning. On Day Two and on all subsequent days of the conclave, two ballots were permitted in the morning session and two more in the afternoon.

For the actual casting of votes, rectangular paper ballots were distributed to the cardinal-electors. On the top half of each ballot was printed the Latin phrase "*Eligo in Summum Pontificem* – I Elect as the Most High Pontiff" with the lower half left blank to insert the name of the preferred candidate. After writing his selection, each cardinal folded the paper twice, walked up to the altar and, holding the ballot up so it could be seen by all, recited, "I call as my witness Christ the Lord who will be my judge, that my vote is given to the one who before God I believe should be elected." He then placed his ballot on a thin gold paten and slid it into a large, bejeweled chalice. When all of the votes had been turned in, they were mixed together by three of the cardinals, designated as cardinal-scrutineers for the conclave, who then counted them to make sure the total matched that of those present. They then read aloud the names on the individual ballots and tallied them. As each ballot was called out, one of the cardinal-scrutineers pierced it with a needle through the word *Eligo* and placed it on a suspended thread so it could be secured against a duplicate count – an ancient but effective safeguard.

If no candidate received the required two-thirds majority needed for election, a second vote immediately followed (except on Day One when only one vote was taken). If there was no winner, all of the ballots from each session's pair of votes – along with the cardinals' handwritten notes – were collected and placed together in a temporary furnace installed specifically for the conclave. The ballots and notes from these unsuccessful votes were then mixed with wet straw and burned to produce dark smoke from the chimney of the Sistine Chapel, thus alerting the gathered faithful in St. Peter's Square that no pope had yet been elected. Sometimes chemicals were added to enhance this blackening effect.

When a candidate finally did receive the requisite two-thirds majority, and thus was to become the next pope, the ballots and notes were burned with *dry* straw, and sometimes with enhancing chemicals, to produce the traditional white smoke proclaiming a new pontiff.

On Day One of the 1958 conclave, Cardinal Ottaviani felt confident, but not with the first ballot. While he had never participated in a previous conclave, having been elevated to the cardinalatial ranks only five years earlier, he assumed that some cardinals might use their initial votes to simply test the waters, or to make a statement. Nonetheless, most of his pre-conclave discussions, especially with his fellow Italian cardinals who comprised the majority of the electors, had given him reason for solid optimism going forward. The five cardinals of the French delegation, however, had seemed particularly brusque and discourteous toward him. While Ottaviani had aggressively pushed the limits of canonical decorum with his probing questioning of most of the newly arriving cardinals, the French had made their own similar, although subtler, entreaties of their foreign peers. While no one currently sequestered within the Sistine Chapel would have remotely ventured that a non-Italian would ever ascend to the Throne of St. Peter, especially after centuries of uninterrupted Italian dominion, symbolic protest votes by the French and others at this early stage of balloting would not be unexpected. Ottaviani was not worried.

The first ballots on Day One were handed in and conscientiously tallied. As expected, Cardinal Siri did well, coming impressively close to a simple majority, although still well short of the two-thirds required for election to the papacy. While it was impossible to know who had voted for which candidate (the cardinals were urged to disguise their handwriting), the portly, aged, affable Italian cardinal from Venice, Angelo Roncalli, had received a surprising number of the initial votes cast. Roncalli was just shy of age seventy-seven, with a reputation as an earthy, non-intellectual but holy man. Ottaviani figured that maybe the French had sent their first votes toward Roncalli as a gesture of thanks for his previous service as the Apostolic Nuncio (papal ambassador) to Paris at the end of World War II. His prospects would surely dissipate as the French and others cast their subsequent votes for a stronger, younger, more electable candidate.

The votes from this first ballot were gathered up by the scrutineers, mixed with wet straw and chemicals, and then burned in the furnace. Very rarely was a pope selected on Day One of a conclave so the dark smoke that ascended from the chimney was not unexpected by those gathered in St. Peter's Square, who were steadily increasing in numbers and settling in for a few long days of prayerful anticipation.

Angelo Giuseppe Roncalli was the fourth of fourteen children born in 1881 to a family of poor tenant farmers in the northern Italian region of Lombardy. As the first-born son, he was expected to remain on the farm and tend the land; however, it was evident early on that he was not suited to the rigorous life unfolding before him. A heavy-set, awkward child, he was given to long, solitary, meandering walks in the fields, lost in contemplative thought, a habit that would center him throughout his life. He cherished the Lombardy plains, its humble, hardworking people, their commonsense approaches to life's challenges, their intense, deeply rooted faith in God. Not surprising to anyone, a religious calling took hold early in Roncalli and he entered the nearby seminary in Bergamo at age eleven. There, he immediately felt at ease. His quiet but welcoming nature, readily proffered smile, self-effacing sense of humor, and a genuine, passionate faith endeared him to fellow students and teachers alike. Nonetheless, while a strong moral conviction was nurtured during these formative years, his academic performance was somewhat unremarkable. After he was ordained a priest in 1904 at age 23, Roncalli spent the next decade as the personal secretary to Giacomo Radini-Tedeschi, the Bishop of Bergamo, Italy, resigning himself to a mundane ecclesiastical career. In 1914, however, that all changed with the advent of World War I. Roncalli was drafted into the Royal Italian Army, serving on the front lines as both a stretcher-bearer and a chaplain. The experience was harrowing for the pacific sharecropper's son; the indescribable horrors of trench warfare he witnessed so close-at-hand would haunt him for the rest of his life.

After the Armistice was signed on November 11, 1918, ending World War I, Roncalli was assigned to Rome and served in a variety of minor bureaucratic posts, eventually being placed in charge of a small department within the Vatican Curia supporting the needs of Catholic missionaries around the globe. He immediately recognized that the strict edicts from his hyper-controlling superiors within the Curia often did more to hamper the missionaries' efforts than to assist them.

For example, the Curia had absolutely no tolerance for incorporating native languages and cultural traditions into local catechisms and the Mass, which was required to be performed in the ancient – and virtually unintelligible to most Catholics – language of Latin. This made practicing their faith far more daunting and unwelcoming than it had to be. Roncalli came across voluminous requests from priests and missionaries around the world asking for flexibility with local rites. He sympathized with their plight and passed along their concerns time and again, verbally and in writing, to his Curial superiors, but to no avail. As a result, their frustration with the outspoken young priest mounted. The consequence for Roncalli was a sudden transfer to the remote Catholic outpost of Bulgaria. While an elevation to the rank of archbishop accompanied the move, it was no small recompense to the disheartened, crestfallen Roncalli. Thus, in 1925 he boarded the Orient Express for Sofia, the first papal representative to set foot in Bulgaria in over 600 years.

Roncalli found himself in a country with only 50,000 Roman Catholics, where the dominant religion was Eastern Orthodox. Furthermore, the embattled King Boris III was embroiled in a bloody civil war, with political assassinations an almost daily occurrence. In fact, within a week of Roncalli's arrival, terrorists bombed the historic St. Nedelya Orthodox Church, killing 150 and wounding 500 more. Roncalli was outraged and immediately undertook to visit all of the victims in area hospitals – an important symbolic gesture that did not go unnoticed by the Bulgarian people as he began navigating the turbulent political and religious waters that were creating tens of thousands of refugees. While very few of the victims were actually Catholic, they became the de facto core of his newfound congregation. He immersed himself in their plight and tended to anyone, regardless of religious affiliation. In the process he developed rapid fluency in the Bulgarian language, furthering his acceptance within the war-torn communities that were in such desperate need. It also cemented his conviction that to truly reach and empathize with a local populace, you had to do so in their own language with sensitivity to their unique customs and traditions.

Yet the young archbishop didn't forget his ecumenical mission to his small but long-neglected Catholic flock. He took on the daunting task of visiting virtually every far-flung parish in the country. He did so by car and train, but just as often by scow and horseback. "Those long-suffering horses that bore me along," he would later recall with a patented smirk, in sympathy to the bulk of their load. "I offered them my prayers, but I'm not sure that lessened their plight."

On all of his parish rounds, Roncalli quickly confirmed the rote superficiality of how the Catholic liturgy was being practiced on a local level outside of Rome. The entire rite of the Mass was in Latin, poorly spoken by local priests, and completely foreign to their congregations who sat there passively and uninvolved throughout each service. Roncalli quietly undertook to personally translate many of the Latin prayers into the Bulgarian language, giving parishioners a newfound and remarkably enthusiastic connection with their faith. These experiences further emphasized to him that the cardinals in the Curia, myopically sequestered within the Vatican walls in Rome, were out of touch with the reality of how Catholicism was being practiced around the world.

Frustrated, he wrote a lengthy letter to his superiors in the Vatican Curia urging that flexibility be allowed to make the Mass more accessible and relevant to local congregations, primarily through the incorporation of local languages. However, he was immediately and aggressively repudiated. Incensed at their refusal to even consider the issue, he penned a passionate letter directly to then Pope Pius XI, the immediate predecessor to Pius XII, expressing these same concerns and suggesting that the Church was missing out on remarkable opportunities to nurture and spread the Catholic faith around the world. Unfortunately for Roncalli, Pius shared the letter with certain powerful members of the Curia, who responded with vitriolic outrage, fiercely denouncing Roncalli's uncalled-for insubordination. Within weeks he was summarily recalled to Rome for an official reprimand. Chastised and humiliated, he returned to Bulgaria convinced that the rest of his pastoral career would likely be spent in remote Italian dioceses from which he could do little further damage.

If that were only so.

Not content to let Roncalli simply languish quietly until retirement, his vindictive superiors in the Curia decided to banish him to Turkey, an even more desolate posting for a Roman Catholic bishop. There, among a total population of 18 million, his Catholic flock would number only 20,000. In addition, he would also be in charge of the Catholic congregations in neighboring Greece, a grand total of 50,000. Roncalli was disconsolate.

Upon his arrival in Istanbul in 1934 at the still relatively young age of fifty-three, Roncalli found that the new political leader of Turkey, Mustafa Kemal Atatürk, had begun a systematic purge of all religions, only tolerating their existence until he could consolidate power, at which time they would be completely eradicated. Atatürk had already prohibited all clerics from wearing any religious garb and assigned spies to follow the most prominent of them, now including Archbishop Roncalli. Suddenly energized into action, Roncalli began meeting covertly with his colleagues from every religious denomination, making secret pacts of unanimity and offering his personal assistance and support. He quietly cultivated relationships with diplomats from many of the foreign embassies in Istanbul, most of whom would soon become valuable sources of intelligence for him, not only on Atatürk but also on the rising threat of Nazi Germany. This became particularly important as rumors began to spread about the systematic rounding up of Jews by the Germans. Through his contacts, Roncalli soon heard of atrocities taking place at what some were calling "death camps." Not waiting for approval from his superiors in Rome, Roncalli immediately took action. He had heard of a small group of nuns in Budapest, Hungary who were quietly forging Catholic baptismal certificates for Jewish families to protect them from deportation. Impressed by their courageous ingenuity, he called in Ira Hirshman of the American War Refugee Board in Turkey and placed in front of him hundreds of official Catholic baptismal certificates, which he had personally signed and endorsed, with the name of the recipient left blank. "Come back for more," Roncalli told Hirshman, "as often as you need. They will be waiting for you." Eventually Roncalli would sign and distribute thousands of fake certificates for Jewish families as well as arrange, through his embassy contacts, exit visas for those who could leave. He secured safe havens for those who could not travel, coordinated emergency food distribution and medical assistance, and led other humanitarian efforts that went well beyond the scope of his ecclesiastical purview. He even intervened with King Boris III of Bulgaria, with whom he had maintained good relations, to cancel deportations of Greek Jews from Bulgaria to Nazi-occupied Greece. Such actions continued throughout the war years, with Roncalli at constant risk of arrest because of his insurgent activities.

Toward the end of World War II, Roncalli was sixty-three years old. Yet he had been reinvigorated. He had clearly become far more independent from his Vatican overseers, working thousands of miles – and cultural leagues – away from the powerful Curia's reach. More importantly, he had come to two profound realizations: first, that cooperation and a true dialogue with other religions was not only possible, but could actually be beneficial for the Roman Catholic Church; and second, that much more could be done to make the individual practice of the Catholic faith more culturally sensitive and thus personally fulfilling for local congregations around the world.

These ideas gelled within him as he was sent on to his next assignment in 1944 to become the Apostolic Nuncio to France, an unexpectedly prominent posting that was quite possibly a form of apology from Pope Pius XII, who was aware of the recently deceased Pope Pius XI's immense regret for not standing up to the Curia when they had so callously exiled Roncalli to Bulgaria and Turkey. Most of

France had been liberated by that time and De Gaulle had come to power, yet there was lingering animosity toward a number of the Catholic Church leaders in France who had not resisted the Vichy government of puppet leader Marshal Petáin and the Nazi-occupiers. Roncalli's calming presence and patient yet firm counsel soon helped mollify tensions between church and state. Most impressive was his subtle easing out of the old-guard cardinals and bishops who had not stood firmly with France in her most urgent time of need. Throughout this process, Roncalli made some incredibly important personal connections with the newly installed Catholic Church hierarchy in France whose promotions he championed. These relationships would soon become disproportionately influential in the upcoming papal conclave.

In 1953, because of his skillful political work in postwar France, Roncalli was finally created a cardinal by Pius XII and named the Patriarch of Venice. At the age of seventy-one, he saw this as a capstone to a remarkably unique career and as a final step toward a peaceful and uneventful retirement.

* * *

Pope Pius XII succumbed on October 9, 1958, at the papal retreat Castel Gandolfo to a debilitating, years-long battle with gastritis. On the night before he died, he asked his housekeeper to open wide the windows to his apartment. As he gazed up to the stars he said quietly, "Look how beautiful, how great is our Lord." Then he closed his eyes and passed gently away in his sleep. Along with his personal physician, his death was confirmed by the Cardinal Camerlengo or Chamberlain, Benedetto Cardinal Masella who, following ancient tradition, gently struck Pius' head with a small silver hammer and called out his Christian name three times. With no response, Cardinal Masella then took possession of the fisherman's ring worn by the pope. The ring, along with the papal seal, was later destroyed in the presence of the College of Cardinals.

As soon as Pius XII was laid to rest two weeks later in the grotto beneath St. Peter's Basilica, intense politicking among the fifty cardinal-electors began in earnest. The Italian cardinals were expected to wield extraordinary influence within the conclave and Cardinal Ottaviani was banking on their solidarity – as well as his formidable sway over them.

Unbeknownst to Ottaviani, however, there was a surprising lack of consensus within the Italian ranks. While he personally relished the possibility of an extended reign for his conservative protege, the young Cardinal Siri, many others were frankly alarmed at the prospect of what could end up being a four-decade-long papacy. However, few of the Italians were willing to outwardly admit any disquiet to Ottaviani before the conclave.

The French, on the other hand, had no such qualms. While they were certainly open to eventually accepting another Italian on the Throne of St. Peter, as had their predecessors for centuries, they similarly had reservations about ceding such a lengthy tenure to any one individual. The French sentiments were also echoed by the three men comprising the American delegation – Francis Cardinal Spellman of New York, James Cardinal McIntyre of Los Angeles, and Edward Cardinal Mooney of Detroit. (Although Cardinal Mooney would be struck by a fatal heart attack only three hours before the conclave was to begin.) The swing votes in the conclave, therefore, at least to Ottaviani's reckoning, were the disparate group of other cardinals from around the world. They were a fractious coalition at best, and to date they had been afforded few real opportunities to get to know each other on a personal basis.

The cardinal-electors were assigned temporary apartments surrounding the Sistine Chapel upon their arrival in Rome. Cardinal Roncalli was given Room #15, which formerly belonged to the Commander of the Noble Guards. An emblazoned plaque "Commandant" appeared above the doorway, a laughable omen thought Roncalli, who was so sure that he was not a realistic candidate for the papacy that he had already purchased his return train ticket to Venice. As soon as all of the cardinals settled in, lobby and hallway discussions of potential papal successors commenced. Outside of the overt posturing by Ottaviani for the candidacy of Cardinal Siri, early talk emerged of a dark horse prospect, Archbishop Giovanni Montini of Milan. No one below the rank of cardinal had been elected pope in over 600 years, although it was indeed a permissible option within canon law. In fact, there were specific procedures to immediately elevate a non-cardinal to the cardinalate within the conclave moments before he would then assume the papacy. However, the lingering talk of Montini's random candidacy, especially at the expense of Cardinal Siri's own prospects, infuriated the quick-tempered Siri so much that he violently punched his fist onto a table, breaking his consecrated cardinal's ruby ring in the process. This incident was recounted widely by the gossiping cardinal-electors and, in a small but potentially significant way, may have turned the tide against the early frontrunner. An ancient adage came to mind: "He who enters the conclave presumed a pope, leaves a cardinal." Siri may have fulfilled his own destiny.

As for Archbishop Montini, his time would indeed come a few years later when he would be elevated to the rank of cardinal and soon thereafter assume the papacy as Pope Paul VI.

———◆———

With the initial inconclusive vote on Day One of the conclave behind them, politicking among the gathered cardinals on the eve of Day Two, October 26, 1958, intensified as the lay of the electoral land began to emerge. While it would have been prohibitively distasteful for Cardinal Siri to lobby on his own behalf, no such restrictions

were placed upon his unabashed advocate. Cardinal Ottaviani was not surprised that the French would put an initial roadblock to any early frontrunner, if for nothing else
than to simply flex some temporary muscle. Therefore,
he concentrated his efforts on the other delegations, primarily those he suspected were more conservative in their
theological leanings. He was confident that many of them
would see the wisdom of following his experienced lead.
For the remainder, he calculated that in the end they would
constitute far less than the one-third necessary to block his
candidate Siri and thus could be ignored.

After a period of debate there were to be two ballots
in the morning session of Day Two, followed if necessary
by a similar afternoon session with two more ballots, and
so forth for continuing days until a candidate had received
the required two-thirds majority. Ottaviani felt certain that
this second day would also be the final day of the conclave.

As the first ballot of the morning was tallied and read
aloud, Ottaviani was encouraged that there was stronger
support for Cardinal Siri than even he had anticipated,
although it was still well short of a two-thirds majority.
While the remaining votes were widely disbursed among
a number of other candidates, including some for Ottaviani himself, momentum finally seemed to be in Siri's favor.
Then, on the second ballot of the morning – the third overall for the conclave – Siri came tantalizingly close to the
requisite two-thirds. Frustrated, yet heartened, Ottaviani
joined his fellow cardinals for the midday recess between
sessions. Feeling extremely optimistic, he relaxed his guard

and did not make any approaches to those he thought were still wavering; he would let the momentum within the conclave take it from there.

As the cardinals filed into the Sistine Chapel for the afternoon session of Day Two, there suddenly seemed to be unexpected enthusiasm for an obscure Armenian Patriarch, Gregorio Pietro Agagianian, of Cilicia. Frustration, especially among the most conservative of the cardinals, began to mount. When the first ballot of Day Two's afternoon session was finally tallied, the sun had already set – as had support for Cardinal Siri, whose numbers had slipped dramatically. Ottaviani seethed at the disloyalty of his peers. A second vote was immediately taken up, with similar results. Contentious rancor enveloped the gathering, startling more than a few of the prelates at the lack of decorum.

As with the previous day's votes, all of the ballots and notes were immediately gathered up by the clearly flustered scrutineers and placed in the furnace. Because of the inconclusive results, the requisite wet straw and appropriate chemicals were supposed to be combined so that black smoke would ascend through the temporary chimney and up to the sky. However, with the intense anger so palpable around him, a beleaguered scrutineer either mixed up the straw or the accompanying chemicals, producing an incorrect plume of white smoke. It was this erroneous plume that had sent the faithful gathered in St. Peter's Square on Day Two of the conclave into a premature frenzy – only to be severely disappointed when the scrutineer suddenly realized his mistake and quickly added the correct mixture of wet straw and chemicals. After a tantalizing few minutes, time enough for even the official Vatican radio announcer to incorrectly proclaim to the world that a new pontiff had been selected, the correct plume of black smoke was finally produced, indicating that a new pope had *not* yet been chosen. The symbolic message, however, that chaos was unfolding within the conclave, could not have been more striking.

That night Ottaviani set to work with intensely renewed resolve – lecturing stalwart colleagues, pleading passionately with others, threatening more than a few. As a result, the next morning, when all of the cardinals filed sleepily back into the Sistine Chapel to begin Day Three of the conclave, he felt warily reassured.

———◆———

Nonetheless, as the votes were tallied for the first morning vote on Day Three, the sixth vote overall, there was a clear indication that Ottaviani's efforts of the previous evening had failed. Support for Cardinal Siri had fallen even farther from its earlier crest, and the second morning ballot showed additional slippage, much to Ottaviani's disgust, which was blatantly obvious to all within the conclave. The ballots and notes were correctly burned, with the resultant black smoke indicating a continuing impasse within the conclave, and the cardinals retreated to their apartments for the midday recess.

Some clear patterns had begun to emerge, however. First and foremost was the feeling among many of the cardinals that a lengthy reign for *any* new pope was not favored, regardless of their theological leanings. As one prelate warily remarked about Cardinal Siri, "He is only fifty-two. He could be pope for the next forty years!" While Ottaviani would certainly have been heartened by such a prospect, his opinion was definitely not shared by his fellow cardinal-electors. In addition, it had become apparent that the French were continuing to vote as a solid bloc for the former Paris diplomat Angelo Cardinal Roncalli, and were now bringing others into their fold. Ottaviani was horrified. He overheard one cardinal crudely remark that he had voted for Roncalli as "someone jolly who will die soon and won't do anything in the meanwhile." As Ottaviani well knew, there was plenty of historical precedent for electing just such a caretaker pope.

When the cardinals gathered in the Sistine Chapel for the afternoon session of Day Three, the debate began to focus on six candidates: Cardinal Siri; Valerio Cardinal Valeri, a conservative colleague of Ottaviani's in the Curia and his strong second preference; Ernesto Cardinal Ruffini of Palermo; Gregorio Pietro Cardinal Agagianian of Armenia; Cardinal Roncalli; and even Cardinal Ottaviani himself. In spite of having four staunch conservatives among those six – Siri, Valeri, Ruffini, Ottaviani – he was worried that they would split the conservative vote. He was right.

It was obvious that the concerns about Cardinal Siri's young age were taking hold. As for Cardinal Valeri, the

French were staunchly against his candidacy. He had been dismissed as the Papal Nuncio to France (and replaced by Roncalli) at the urging of De Gaulle because of his collaboration with the Vichy regime during World War II. As for Cardinal Ruffini, his leadership of the Archdiocese of Palermo had been marred by persistent rumors concerning his relationship with the Mafia. And Ottaviani was simply too polarizing of a figure, despite a small but voraciously loyal following.

As the cardinals opened the afternoon session of Day Three with the first vote, their eighth overall, a remarkably unforeseen race suddenly took shape between two of the longest shots entering the conclave: Cardinal Agagianian of Armenia, the first serious non-Italian papal candidate in centuries; and Cardinal Roncalli of Venice. The second vote confirmed that parallel outcome. Ballots were burned signaling no papal successor had yet been chosen but the cardinals exited the Sistine Chapel with a universal sense of anticipation that the end of the conclave was finally in sight.

<hr />

That night of informal discussions within the papal apartments was telling. One by one, cardinals stopped by Roncalli's room to speak quietly with him, to get a firmer sense of his theological leanings, to not-so-subtly gauge his health status. On the eve of potentially the most important day of his life, one which he would have rather spent alone in prayerful meditation, Roncalli was constantly interrupted by knocks on his door. This continued well into the night. Finally, after a mere hour or two of fitful sleep, a clearly exhausted Cardinal Roncalli joined his colleagues in the morning as they processed into the Sistine Chapel for Day Four of their deliberations. It was Tuesday, October 28, 1958.

What became immediately apparent in that morning's first vote was that Cardinal Agagianian of Armenia was not a serious final contender. His non-Italian heritage, even though he had spent a majority of his adult life in Rome, clearly hindered his chances. The true surprise was that it had now suddenly become a *different* two-man race – between Cardinal Roncalli, who had garnered twenty of the necessary thirty-four votes on the first morning ballot, and Cardinal Ottaviani, who had picked up much of the previous support for Agagianian. With fifteen votes cast for Ottaviani's candidacy, it appeared that the conservative bloc was coalescing behind him. But was it too late? The ballots were immediately distributed for the second morning vote. An almost unbearable intensity enveloped the Sistine Chapel as each cardinal bowed their head in prayerful deliberation as they filled in their choice. Ottaviani suddenly allowed himself to consider the previously unthinkable. Could *he* become the next pope? By what name should he be called? He hadn't even entertained such a prospect and was thus completely (and uncharacteristically) unprepared.

As each cardinal slowly rose from his chair, carried his ballot up to the altar, and gently slid it into the chalice, a suffocating quiet overtook the room. The tallying commenced.

The cardinal-scrutineers read aloud the name on each individual ballot – slowly, deliberately, momentously – and the results soon became evident. On the eleventh overall ballot of the conclave, Angelo Cardinal Roncalli of Venice, a month shy of his seventy-seventh birthday, had been elected as the new pope. The final tally: Roncalli - 38, Ottaviani - 9, with the remaining votes interspersed.

All eyes locked on Roncalli as he haltingly, ponderously, made his way to the altar and sat somewhat awkwardly upon the papal throne. Cardinal Tisserant, the Cardinal Dean, then approached him and asked, in the same manner as popes had been asked for centuries, "Do you accept your canonical election as Supreme Pontiff?" Roncalli responded with a serene, barely audible, "Yes." Tisserant then asked, "By what name do you wish to be called?" To this, Roncalli pulled out a handwritten paper that he had tucked into his cassock pocket in the wee hours of the morning. "I choose John," he read, "a name sweet to me because it is the name of my father, dear to me because it is the name of the humble parish church where I was baptized. It is the solemn name of numberless cathedrals scattered throughout the world, including our own basilica St. John Lateran. Twenty-two Johns of indisputable legitimacy have been pope, and almost all had a brief pontificate." At this last statement, he looked up at his fellow cardinals, acknowledging that he understood full well why he had been chosen.

With that proclamation, each of the cardinals lowered their canopies in deference and came forward, one by one, to pledge their fealty to Pope John XXIII. The last to do so was Alfredo Cardinal Ottaviani.

<hr/>

As the unmistakable white smoke was dissipating above St. Peter's Basilica to the resounding cheers of the gathered faithful, the new pope was led by Cardinal Tisserant to the Room of Tears, just a few feet away from the Sistine Chapel. It was thus called because for centuries newly elected popes, overwhelmed by the joy as well as the burden of their pending station, were known to shed tears there just moments before being presented to the awaiting throng in Saint Peter's Square. In the room was a selection of papal vestments in three sizes – small, medium and large – because the identity of the new pope was not known by the Vatican tailors beforehand. Unfortunately, they had not expected so portly of a new pontiff. Pope John shimmied and squeezed into the largest of the available vestments, chose a more fitting pair of shoes and white cap, then followed Cardinal Tisserant out onto the balcony of St. Peter's Basilica. When the two men became visible to the thousands of faithful below, a deafening roar erupted that lasted for close to ten minutes. When Cardinal Tisserant was finally able to speak he proclaimed, "*Annuntio vobis gaudium magnum* – I announce to you a great joy," and drowned out among the euphoria, "*Habemus papam!* – We have a pope!"

Among the multitude in St. Peter's Square was a brash, ambitious Irish-American priest, Father Francis Xavier Murphy.

"I'll be *damned*," he muttered upon seeing who had been chosen. "I'll…be…*damned!*"

CHAPTER II

———◆———

"A Council!"

F ather Francis Xavier Murphy was a Roman Catholic Redemptorist priest who was totally in his
element in Rome. He loved church history and was
a gifted writer, two passions that would soon coalesce to
make him one the most prolific religious authors of his day
and – some would argue – easily the most controversial.
He was fluidly self-assured, with an exuberant humor and
a dashing charm that was immediately endearing to most.

Murphy was stocky, of medium height, with a combed-
back shock of wavy light brown hair. His piercing blue eyes
betrayed a keen intelligence. He had a photographic memory for names and the personal details of those he came
across. Without question, he was a people person, always
in the company of others for an early morning espresso, a
lingering late lunch, or drinks and dinner that inevitably
extended into the wee hours of the morning. He also had
an uncanny, and not coincidental, knack for befriend-
ing those with influence – political, social, and certainly

religious, the latter often overlapping with the previous two. He relished gossip; he loved conflict; he was unwavering in his convictions.

———————◆———————

Murphy was born in the Bronx in 1914 to rebellious parents who had eloped from County Clare in Ireland against their family's wishes. Upon first arriving in the United States, his father, Dennis Murphy, moved from odd job to odd job, never earning a reliable source of steady income and often spending much of what he did earn at one of the innumerable New York immigrant Irish taverns, drinking heavily and spinning yarns late into the night. Through the persistent coercion of his increasingly frustrated wife Anna (née Rynne), Dennis reluctantly applied to become a New York City policeman. He was initially rejected because he was two years over the maximum entry age of twenty-six, but Anna, undeterred, had a baptismal certificate forged by a newly ordained (and likely intimidated) young priest to falsely show a later date of birth. That was sufficient proof of age for an unsuspecting enlisting officer at a different precinct, and Dennis was finally accepted into New York's Finest.

Once Dennis was on a regular payroll, and thus working much of the time, Anna turned their home into a boarding house in order to earn extra income for the family, which now included their son Frank and two other children, Patricia and Annabelle. With its fortuitous location in the shadows of the newly-built Yankee Stadium, the house's weekly rentals soon evolved into a reasonably profitable enterprise. At an early age, young Murphy was able to rub elbows with many of the visiting young ballplayers of the day who, trying to save money on their meager salaries, became regular boarders when in town. (A further attraction of the house for the players was the constant flow of newly-arrived Irish lasses seeking inexpensive lodging until they secured employment opportunities in the city.)

Murphy was mesmerized by the wildly-embellished stories of each player's accomplishments, both on and off the field, clearly intended to sway the interests of the impressionable female newcomers – and with impressive levels of late-night romantic success, much of which Murphy surreptitiously observed. In the subsequent mornings, one of his household responsibilities was to then escort the young women throughout Manhattan while they searched for jobs, often taking extra time to show them the sights of the burgeoning metropolis. The ladies' detailed recounting of the previous night's exploits, along with highly suggestive flirtations toward the young teenager, made Murphy's task more than acceptable to him, something that did not go unnoticed by his autocratic mother.

<hr>

In spite of those adolescent yearnings, or likely because of them, an early vocation to the priesthood for Murphy was strongly encouraged, actually mandated, by his devoutly Catholic matriarch. Thus, at the formative age of fourteen, he was sent off to a rural Redemptorist order minor seminary in northeast Pennsylvania.

Murphy was indeed a religious child, never complaining about going to Mass on Sundays, seemingly looking forward to it. Furthermore, when the family read the Bible together each night, the young Murphy was always a willing participant, taking a particularly keen interest in the ancient passages of the Old Testament.

In many ways, Murphy looked upon the seminary as an adventure, made all the more appealing by its bucolic setting that was in such stark contrast to the dirty, rat-infested Bronx neighborhood that was all he had ever known.

Murphy's self-confidence and easygoing temperament also made the adjustment surprisingly smooth. He immediately became the rollicking leader of the first-year teenage seminarians, most of them desperately homesick, many of them sent there unwillingly at the behest of often overbearing or overly-zealous Catholic parents. He led impromptu (usually unauthorized) forays into the nearby town, organized teams for baseball, staged canoe races and other games, set up elaborate pranks, and snuck out of seminary windows past curfew on more than a few occasions to visit nearby summer camps and boarding schools for girls.

Murphy was revered by his peers for his pluck and enthusiasm, making an initially intolerable transition for many of the young men more bearable. Nonetheless, a good number of his classmates left during that first year;

others had no recourse but to stay, internally suffering and seething at their inexorable fate toward what they viewed as an unfulfilling career in the priesthood. Not Frank Murphy.

———— ◆ ————

Overlooking his obvious lack of discipline, Murphy's seminarian superiors saw something special in him – a remarkably keen, inquisitive, relatively untapped yet intrepid intelligence – not to mention an exceptional gift for writing in a boy his age.

He had always been a good student, albeit somewhat belligerent and ill-behaved in class. But he read voraciously: the newspaper, adventure books, sports stories, biographies, the Bible, and especially history. Frank read anything he could get his hands on, borrowing books incessantly, re-reading them often. Yet it wasn't until he arrived at the seminary that he was required to actually *write* to any significant extent. It was amazing how much he had gleaned from the writing styles of so many diverse authors. His vocabulary was expansive, his rhetoric nuanced yet powerful, his arguments factual and persuasive, his research carefully cultivated and comprehensive. Beyond the formulaic curriculum of the seminary, he often delved independently and passionately into the obscurest of subjects related to ancient church history, something anathema to even the most diligent of his fellow students.

When Murphy next moved on to the Redemptorist major seminary in Esopus, New York in 1940, where he would take his final vows as an ordained priest, he had already published his first scholarly article – on the life works of Saint Jerome.

He then continued his studies at Catholic University in Washington, DC, earning a Ph.D. in 1945 with a thesis on the 4th-century theologian Rufinus of Acquileia. After a brief stint as a chaplain at the United States Naval Academy in Annapolis, he returned to Esopus as a teacher and continued writing extensively on ancient church history. In 1948, his growing body of published work caught the attention of academics within the Redemptorist headquarters in Rome, where there was a long-overdue need to catalogue the order's vast archives. It was an excruciatingly mundane task, but it turned out to be an opportunity the young priest relished – not only for the order's rich historical trove but also for the chance to explore Rome itself. In fact, his move to Rome was the first trip of more than a few hundred miles Murphy had ever taken beyond his native Bronx.

<hr />

Italy at the time was in the beginning throes of its long, post-World War II political disarray and news outlets were scrambling to make sense of it all. Almost immediately upon his arrival in Rome, Murphy was approached by a Catholic news service and asked to put aside his archival duties to cover the chaotic 1948 Italian elections. He jumped at the opportunity, whetting an appetite for confrontational politics that would continue unabated for the rest of his life.

This first journalistic foray put Murphy in direct contact with not only a bevy of Italian political hopefuls but also with many higher-ups within the Vatican leadership who were closely monitoring the Italian elections. Notably, Murphy met numerous times with Monsignors Domenico Tardini and Giovanni Montini (the future Pope Paul VI), who co-ran the Vatican's Secretariat of State, as well as with a legion of lower-level church bureaucrats whose insider knowledge of Vatican machinations added invaluable depth to his reporting. Of the latter group, by far the most important was Montini's personal secretary, Monsignor Giovanni Benelli, who in the years ahead would become a priceless if mostly anonymous covert Vatican source for Murphy.

Overall, this was extraordinary access for an ambitious young journalist/priest, something he would tap into again and again in the coming years.

In 1951, at the onset of the Korean War, Murphy volunteered for service in the U.S. Army. Returning from Rome to an initial assignment at Fort Riley in Kansas, he was soon deployed as a field chaplain to the Korean theater, where he saw action on the front lines and earned a Bronze Star. However, beyond the battlefield Murphy witnessed rampant, racially-motivated disciplinary actions toward enlisted servicemen.

Never one to shy away from a perceived injustice or from personally taking action to address it, Murphy repeatedly confronted his commanding officers. When they did not address the issues, at least not to his satisfaction, Murphy's antagonizing persistence led to him being summarily transferred out of his unit and reassigned to France.

There he first met Archbishop Angelo Roncalli, the future Pope John XXIII, who impressed him with his calmly persistent ability to ease smoldering tensions between the Catholic hierarchy in France and the De Gaulle government.

<hr />

After only a few short months in France, however, Murphy was transferred once again, this time to Germany. In addition to his pastoral duties with the troops, a disproportionate amount of his time was taken up counseling desperate German women whose children had been fathered – and then abandoned – by American GIs during their tours of duty. With no means of support, and with both mother and child cruelly ostracized by an intolerant German society, these children were being orphaned with heartbreaking regularity.

Initially by default, and then out of compassionate rage, Murphy became personally involved with many of their cases, trying unsuccessfully to track down the fathers, contacting already-overburdened relief organizations to no avail, and getting absolutely no help from uncooperative German social service agencies.

Finally, with no chance of resolution through traditional channels, he began an exhaustive writing campaign to family and friends back in the United States describing the crisis and asking for help. To his surprise, first one, and then a growing number of childless American couples began contacting him directly, having heard of a certain "resourceful" priest in Germany who might be able to facilitate a "streamlined" adoption process. In fact, one initial couple offered a remarkably generous stipend to quietly compensate him for his efforts, to be used "in any way deemed necessary." Murphy pounced on the opportunity. After a few well-placed "inducements," certain individuals within overwhelmed relief organizations and an occasional government bureaucrat or two were suddenly more than willing to pass along abandoned children to welcoming American families with minimal paperwork and delay. Murphy then proffered that same template to other anxious couples in the States and soon a remarkably efficient, if not quasi-illegal, adoption channel was launched. In Murphy's eyes, this was a win-win situation on every level, not to mention giving him unencumbered access to a significant accumulation of leftover – and, more importantly – unaccounted for, funds. When off duty or on leave, he took much of that surplus money and traveled widely (and quite extravagantly for a typical priest) until his final military transfer back to the United States in 1957 as the base chaplain at Fort Hamilton in Brooklyn, New York.

Upon his discharge from the Army in 1958, Murphy was assigned to a working-class Redemptorist parish in the Bronx near his childhood home; however, he longed for a return to the excitement of Europe. For months he pushed for a transfer and, when a research position suddenly opened up at the Redemptorist Accademia Alfonsiana in Rome, he aggressively – and successfully – pursued it. His timing could not have been more fortuitous. Shortly after his arrival he found himself in the piazza fronting St. Peter's on that historic sunlit day of October 28, 1958, where he witnessed the acclamation for the new Pope John XXIII.

Immediately after Pope John gave his first blessing from the balcony of St. Peter's Basilica, the new pope returned to the Sistine Chapel where the cardinals were awaiting the official closing of the papal conclave. During his brief absence, there had been stunned silence. The reality of that historic moment, of the new papacy, of their collective fateful decision, was suddenly upon them. To a man, they all assumed that John's would be a short-lived, uneventful pontificate, simply marking time until a strong, dynamic, younger new pope would be called upon to lead the Church through this troubling era. Pope John clearly shared that belief himself.

In opposite corners of the Sistine Chapel were Cardinals Ottaviani and Siri, now awkwardly set far apart after their intimate collusion during the preceding days of deliberations. Ottaviani was still fuming; Siri was more resolute, keeping in mind that there would indeed be another chance, likely *chances*, for his own elevation to the papacy in the not-too-distant future.

As Pope John, followed by Cardinal Tisserant, re-entered the Sistine Chapel from the basilica's balcony, he was greeted by warm, bona fide applause. He raised his hand to quiet his colleagues and then made a surprising request, asking them all to remain in conclave with him until the next morning instead of following tradition and allowing them to leave immediately for their respective homes. The new pope was a man who always felt most comfortable with and among people and he suddenly felt very alone; he simply wanted their company, their comradery, before the station of his new office inevitably changed their relationships forever. Although puzzled, the cardinals to a man of course acquiesced.

Then, all of a sudden, Monsignor Tardini and a trio of other Vatican officials, close friends of the former Angelo Roncalli but not among the cardinals in conclave, came bursting forth into the Sistine Chapel, unaware that the inviolability of the conclave was still in effect. As they rushed in to enthusiastically congratulate the new pope, they were abruptly stopped short by the shrieking, almost hysterical voice of Cardinal Tisserant, who accused them of breaching the sacredness of the conclave. Turning to Monsignor Tardini in particular, the Cardinal Dean shouted, "You are now *immediately excommunicated!*" Shocked at the implication of Tisserant's remarkable declaration, they slinked away and quickly exited. All of the cardinals were stunned, as was Pope John himself, clearly uncertain how to proceed. After an extremely uncomfortable few minutes, without the intervention of the dumbfounded new pope, the cardinals quietly filtered out of the Chapel, the warmth and tenor of that potentially poignant moment with the new pope now completely destroyed.

That night Pope John did not wait for knocks on his apartment door. He made the rounds himself, chatting with old friends, cementing new relationships. The casualness of the atmosphere was welcome, allowing the tensions of the conclave to dissipate. He eventually stopped by the apartment of Cardinal Ottaviani, who was alone and brooding when Pope John knocked on his door and was bade to enter. He noticed that Ottaviani had shut his window in a vain attempt to keep out the noise of the celebratory crowd below in St. Peter's Square. They exchanged brief, uncomfortable yet polite, remarks, then John quipped, calling upon his peasant roots, "For a farmer, next year will always be better." Ottaviani smiled wanly as Pope John left his room, then pondered the meaning of those words more warily. *Better for whom?* he thought.

The new pope continued visiting his brethren until just before sunrise, when he finally retired to Room 15 for the last time. He stopped at the sign adjacent to the door that read "Commandant" and laughed at what had turned out to be a prescient omen. He then entered his apartment, opened the window, and let in the cool, invigorating October breeze. He looked down upon the now nearly-empty piazza, knelt at the windowsill and prayed, the enormity of the moment finally cascading upon him.

———◆———

The next morning, in his first official act as Pope John XXIII, he gathered all of the cardinals together for Mass at the high altar in St. Peter's Basilica, after which he formally closed the conclave. He then received each cardinal individually to give them a special blessing, extend his gratitude, and promise his dutiful stewardship on their behalf.

As his second official act, he called Monsignor Tardini and his overzealous colleagues into his new papal office, austere and spartan with the removal of his predecessor's personal furnishings. With mock seriousness, Pope John lifted the penalty of excommunication imposed on them by Cardinal Tisserant the previous day. They laughed, clearly relieved, and enjoyed a warm, informal moment of shared excitement with their friend. It was relationships such as these that the pope had cultivated and cherished over the years but would soon find more challenging to sustain in his role as Supreme Pontiff. His relationship with Monsignor Tardini, in particular, was especially heartfelt, and John asked him to remain behind after the others departed.

Back in 1944, while in charge of foreign affairs for the Vatican Secretariat of State, Tardini had been directly involved in getting Pope John, then Archbishop Roncalli in Turkey, his posting to Paris. However, he had not been

Tardini's first pick, or second, or even third. When Roncalli learned of this, he wrote in his acceptance letter to Tardini, "Where there are not horses available, the donkeys trot along." This broke the ice in what could have been an awkward start to a relationship that soon evolved into an extraordinarily cooperative and highly effective diplomatic partnership. This was particularly important in the post-World War II transition period in France, when Roncalli's amiable personality and Tardini's intimate knowledge of Vatican machinations collaborated to guide the Catholic hierarchy in France through some potentially calamitous political minefields during the new De Gaulle regime.

As Monsignor Tardini stayed behind in Pope John's office on that first day of the new papacy, he anticipated what was going to be asked of him and tried to head it off. "Holy Father, I am seventy years old and I am tired. My fervent wish is to devote my remaining time on God's earth to the orphanage of Villa Nazareth, a cause that I have championed for years." Tardini bowed his head and waited.

Pope John had already foreseen this. "It is easier for a father to have children than for children to have a real father," he began in his folksy way, "especially in such troubled times as these." John paused, sighed, then continued, almost plaintively. "Please know that I understand. I hear you. But I also need you." John looked intently at Tardini, whose head was still bowed. "As my own father used to say, anyone can farm, but not everyone is a farmer." Tardini looked up with a quizzical glance. "My dear friend, anyone can be an ambassador," John continued, "but few can do so with diplomacy. I want you, I need you, to serve as my Secretary of State."

"And what of Monsignor Montini?" Tardini asked on behalf of his long-time colleague in the Secretariat of State.

For years, Tardini, along with Monsignor Giovanni Montini (the future Pope Paul VI), had effectively shared the day-to-day running of the Vatican Secretariat of State in the absence of an appointed cardinal as its head. Both had performed exceptionally well in their respective roles. "He will be elevated to the rank of cardinal. As will you. I will put him in charge of the Diocese of Milan." And then John added with a laugh, "You will be in charge of the world."

Both Tardini and Montini had previously been offered cardinalships by Pope Pius XII but had turned them down, a rare and truly remarkable act of humility on their parts. Now the red caps would be tendered a second time. While Tardini's inclination was once again to refuse, there was something different about this pope. Something disarming, something imperceptibly beguiling. "As you wish, Holy Father," the soon-to-be Cardinal Tardini reluctantly replied.

Pope John was more sympathetic to Tardini's retirement wish than he let on. The problem with orphans in Italy was acute in the post-World War II years, where hundreds of thousands of fathers had been either killed in battle or been captured and eventually died in Russian gulags. To make matters worse, Pope Pius XII, at the behest of hardline cardinals in the Curia in 1946, had issued a papal directive that all Jewish children in Europe who were "unofficially baptized" during the war, albeit for their own protection against Nazi deportation to concentration camps, were *not* to be taken in by Catholic families and charities, including orphanages. Pope John, then Angelo Roncalli as the Apostolic Nuncio in France at the time, was aghast and he blatantly ignored the directive, which would have affected tens of thousands of children in post-war France.

Furthermore, the total collapse of the Italian economy in the decades after the war had continued to result in additional thousands of abandoned children, many ashamedly dropped off in already overcrowded orphanages by desperate mothers unable to care for them. Pope John was extremely sensitive to their plight. Therefore, it was with truly mixed emotions that he requested the services of now-Cardinal Tardini to be his Secretary of State at the expense of his commitment to the orphanage at Villa Nazareth.

The first few weeks of John's new papacy were scripted in minute detail. Lengthy, legally arcane documents needed to be signed; a constant stream of introductory audiences with diplomats were required as they presented their credentials to the new pontiff; long-pending Vatican vacancies awaited his approval. It was time-consuming and sometimes overwhelming for the new pope. Then there were the requisite official rituals of the office; some very public, such as the traditional Wednesday blessing of the faithful gathered in St. Peter's Square, others privately intrusive. For example, by tradition popes were supposed to dine alone, something that rankled the highly personable John. Within the first week, that practice changed, much to the chagrin of the protocol staff within the Curia. An invitation to a meal with Pope John soon became a commonplace occurrence for a wide range of Vatican staffers – and not just the ecclesiastical elite.

John was also frustrated that his daily routine was being scheduled without his prior input or approval. He therefore began to spontaneously venture outside the walls of Vatican City – vexing Curial officials and security personnel alike – to simply walk among the people who lived and worked in the shadows of St. Peter's. One evening he even made an impromptu visit to Rome's infamous central prison, Regina Coeli, which harbored some of the most notorious inmates in all of Italy. After making his way through the various guard stations, he entered the cavernous central atrium, surrounded on all sides and on five levels by rust-covered, iron-barred cells. "It was easier for me to visit you than for you to visit me!" he called out to the surprised prisoners. The resultant laughter was resounding. When it finally died down, he asked them to bow their heads in prayer and gave them a special blessing. Then, as he turned to leave, the prison erupted in echoing applause. It reminded John of similar visits he had made years earlier to political prisons in Bulgaria and Turkey.

Later that same night, after returning to the Vatican, the new pope secretly slipped into the vacant, eerily quiet Vatican Museum to view one of his favorite masterworks, Raphael's *The Liberation of St. Peter*. Painted in 1514, the three-paneled fresco illustrated the story of St. Peter's deliverance from prison as recounted in the New Testament: "Behold, an angel of the Lord appeared, and a light shone in the cell; and he struck Peter on the side and woke him, saying, 'Get up quickly.' And the chains fell off his hands."

The triptych told the story of three distinct episodes taken from the Acts of the Apostles. The left panel depicted the confusion of the guards; the second, the appearance of the Angel of Freedom in St. Peter's cell; the third, Peter, now unchained, being led to freedom by the hand of the divine messenger.

The middle panel, in particular, had resonance for Pope John. Raphael portrayed the angel arriving in a brilliant burst of light above a prostrate St. Peter; however, the image was partially obscured behind grilled prison bars. Raphael had painted the triptych in homage to his patron, Pope Julius II, whose papacy was marred by Vatican infighting and political turmoil. And yet, as Raphael alluded in the third panel, there would eventually be a way out for the beleaguered Julius in his quest to restore the Papal States, which had been reduced to ruin by the infamous Borgia family.

What message does this have for me? John pondered as he gazed up at the painting in the muted light and solitude of the empty museum. *What chains, what bars, will I have to overcome? And to what end?*

A few days later, Pope John held the first-ever Vatican press conference by a sitting pontiff. The reporters were uncertain how to react to this novel opportunity and their initial questions were hesitant and superficial. When one reporter asked, "How many people work at the Vatican?" Pope John replied, "About half." After a lingering pause, taken by complete surprise at a pope with a sense of humor, the room erupted in laughter. A warm and mutually respectful relationship with the press had thus been established – something that would become invaluable to Pope John in the next few years as a simmering, revolutionary idea began to germinate in his mind after that late-night visit to Raphael's prescient fresco.

While Pope John came across as politely affable and unassuming, at his core he was a man of fierce and determined action. Nonetheless, if there was anyone in Rome who thought that he was facing a short-lived pontificate, it was certainly John himself. Therefore, he didn't have time to waste.

As a first step, he took what most Church insiders acknowledged was a long overdue action to bring the College of Cardinals up to its historic number of seventy, a decreed level set by Pope Sixtus V back in 1590. The current number was only fifty. John asked the Curia to prepare a list of potential candidates for elevation, which they promptly submitted – and which, upon reviewing, John immediately rejected. With the clear imprint of Cardinal Ottaviani's handiwork, the candidates were uniformly ultra-conservative and virtually all Italian. This would not do. He went back and asked for a roster of *all* eligible bishops from throughout the world and then personally culled that list for specific traits, most notably independence of thought and geographic diversity. He soon nominated twenty-three new cardinals, thirteen of whom were from Italy. Not ideal, he thought, but it was a start. In the coming year he would elevate another twenty-nine additional cardinals, only nine of whom would be Italian-born. The cardinals in the Curia protested vigorously when they saw the register of his proposed appointments, especially when the College of Cardinals would now exceed seventy, potentially diluting their considerable sway. Cardinal Ottaviani, in particular, was apoplectic, ranting from office to office throughout the meandering Vatican corridors. When Pope John heard of this, he simply laughed and retorted with a wry smile, "But Sixtus had a smaller flock to tend," a riposte that was duly passed on to the still-seething Ottaviani. Pope John had made his first move against the power of the Curia. It would not be his last.

With the expanded College of Cardinals, Pope John was also looking to provide more opportunities for the newcomers' direct participation in Vatican affairs, another strike at the entrenched Curial power base. Most of the cardinals currently leading the dozen or so congregations within the Curia, equivalent to cabinet departments, had been in their positions for decades. And some, most notably Cardinal Tisserant, the elderly Dean of the College of Cardinals, actually had two *different* congregations under his sole purview. The Curial leadership was determined not to relinquish even minimal control, unanimous in their defiance of the new pope.

Yet John was just as determined. He summoned into his personal office both Cardinals Tisserant and Ottaviani, the most outspoken ringleaders of the Curial rebellion. They entered confidently, combative, certain that they would prevail over this impetuous Vatican outsider.

"Please sit," Pope John said formally, and with a wry smile, as he pointed to the simple wooden chairs around his spartan desk. They both, however, continued to stand, somewhat surprised that the length of the meeting would necessitate this. "Please," John said again, this time more firmly, and they finally did so.

John then took his own seat behind his desk and began speaking of the need to welcome some of their new cardinal peers into leadership posts within the Curia. Cardinal Ottaviani immediately stood up, intending to interrupt, but he was cut short by the raising of the pope's right hand. He sat back down, John paused, then continued.

"I am asking each of you to relinquish your leadership positions," John said directly and firmly, with an unexpected boldness. "And I will ask the same of your Curial brethren."

Both cardinals were shocked. They stared back in broiling silence. Then, remarkably, they looked at each other, stood up in unison on their own accord, bowed ever-so-slightly to Pope John, and simply walked out. John sat there stunned at their arrogance, their callous disrespect – if not for him personally then for the mantle that he wore, the papacy itself. John became uncharacteristically enraged, calling out for his new Secretary of State, Cardinal Tardini, who shuffled in warily from the adjoining anteroom.

"Ottaviani and Tisserant refused me! They refused!" Pope John shouted at Tardini, fuming at their outrageous behavior. "Never in my life did I think anyone would refuse the pope!"

Not at all surprised by the contemptuous actions of his well-entrenched peers but yet still with a simmering anger of his own toward Cardinal Tisserant for his short-lived "excommunication" of him during the conclave, Tardini thought for a moment and then proposed a compromise. "Since Cardinal Tisserant is the head of both the Congregation for the Oriental Churches and also the Vatican Library, why not first send a message to the Curia by officially taking at least one of *his* away." A vindictive smirk crossed Tardini's lips as he said this.

Pope John thought for a moment, nodded, then smiled sardonically in return.

"And Cardinal Ottaviani's turn will indeed come as well," Tardini added.

"Yes indeed," John responded. "For everything there is a season. A time to tear down … and a time to build."

The next day Pope John called Cardinal Tisserant back into his office, this time alone. Not even giving the elderly dean a chance to sit down, he just stated flatly, "You will remain as head of the Vatican Library but no longer the Congregation of the Oriental Churches." Not expecting any response, and not receiving one, John continued, "Effective immediately."

Flabbergasted, Tisserant stared mutely at Pope John for a remarkably long time, weighing whether to verbalize to the pope what was truly on his mind. He refrained, however, almost to Pope John's disappointment. Then he bowed stiffly, turned, and walked out. A knavish smile crossed Pope John's face. *Maybe the Curia was not so all-powerful after all,* he thought, perhaps naively.

News of Cardinal Tisserant's demotion by Pope John spread rapidly through the Vatican corridors. However, rather than acquiescing to the new pope, the cardinals of the Curia hardened their resolve. Unbeknownst to them, so had Pope John.

With the first weeks of his papacy behind him, Pope John continued with most of the scripted meetings and events on his daily schedule, but he started to reserve extended time in each day for personal prayer and contemplation. The burden of his office, of the papacy, was already becoming overwhelming, almost unbearable. Furthermore, the world around him was in crisis, with revolutions taking hold from Cuba to Africa, nuclear escalation between the United States and the Soviet Union continuing unabated, a nascent conflict in Vietnam unfolding, and widespread societal unrest infiltrating the younger generation.

The Catholic Church was certainly not immune to what was going on in the world. How would the Church itself be impacted? How would it survive? John began to take long, pensive, meandering walks throughout the beautiful Vatican gardens, as popes had similarly done over the millennia since Pope Nicholas III had moved the papal residence back to the Vatican from the Lateran Palace in 1277, almost 700 years ago.

John often stopped at the towering statue of St. Peter in the center of the gardens, pausing literally and figuratively in the shadow of that very first pope, a tangible, intimidating reminder of whose mantle he had so unexpectedly inherited. Peter, in magnificent profile, was perpetually reaching toward the grand basilica that bore his name. John loved to stand on the walkway behind the statue, sharing the same view as Peter, framed by the ever-changing bluish hues of the Roman sky. Throughout all of his trials, St. Peter stood majestically there, unflinching, unencumbered, looking up to the heavens.

One afternoon as Pope John strolled contemplatively past the imposing statue, enumerating in his mind the incalculable issues facing his Church – and thus himself – he gazed down at an almost hidden, verdigris-covered plaque at the statue's base commemorating the only Ecumenical Council to ever be held at the Vatican itself. It was also the most recent – in 1869. John thought pensively for a moment, then looked up, following St. Peter's outstretched arm and gazing toward the cloud-filtered light streaming behind the basilica's monumental dome that had beckoned the faithful from around the world for centuries. He suddenly came to a startling epiphany.

A Council, Pope John thought to himself. *A Council...*

In the 2,000-year history of the Catholic Church, there had only been twenty such Ecumenical (Universal) Councils, starting with the Council of Nicaea in 325, which proclaimed the true divinity of Jesus as the Son of God. Prior to the Vatican Council of 1869, which had promulgated the infallibility of the Pope on ultimate matters of Christian doctrine, the next preceding Council was back in 1545, when the Council of Trent had condemned the edicts of Martin Luther and other reformers.

A Council... What if he called another Ecumenical Council to bring together all of the cardinals and bishops from throughout the world to discuss the problems now facing the Church? A Council to help him shoulder this immense burden that had so unwillingly been thrust upon him?

John quickly shuffled back toward his office where he immediately summoned Cardinal Tardini, who had become one of his few trusted advisors. When Tardini entered, he found the pope pacing in surprisingly fluid animation for his heavy-set frame.

Pope John didn't wait for Tardini to sit down but began detailing a number of seemingly intractable crises facing the Catholic Church: a disaffected laity, due in no small measure to the mandatory use of Latin in all religious services; the iron-fisted, myopic power hold of the Vatican Curia; the absence of any meaningful dialogue with other religions; the Church virtually ignoring contemporary societal issues at its own peril. The new pope went on and on. To each point, Tardini cautiously nodded his agreement. Then, with almost childlike enthusiasm, Pope John asked, "Well, what do you think can be done?"

After a lengthy pause, Tardini sheepishly replied, "To be honest, Holy Father, I do not know."

"Neither do I," responded Pope John, with a hearty chuckle. "Therefore, I have an idea." He looked directly at Tardini to gauge his response as he blurted out, "A Council!"

Not sure what reaction to expect from such a radical idea, John was relieved when Tardini, after waiting pensively for a few seconds, responded with an almost imperceptible nod. "Yes. Yes," he whispered. "A Council."

It had been less than two months since Pope John had ascended to the Throne of St. Peter. A revolution was about to begin.

CHAPTER III

"A brilliant gambit"

ather Murphy had settled into a spartan apartment at the Accademia Alfonsiana, which included a small closet, twin bed, tall dresser, unmatched wooden desk and chair, and a tarnished but functional brass lamp. A single window overlooked a large interior courtyard, a quarter of which was used as a private, off-street parking lot. The rest of the quadrangle was comprised of well-manicured shrubs and narrow walkways dotted with religious statuary.

Murphy had already gotten to know many of his fellow Redemptorist priests who were stationed there in various capacities – some with teaching positions as visiting scholars, others as researchers and archivists like Murphy, and still others as administrators for the Redemptorist order's headquarters next door. Among them was Father André Sampers, who had arrived at the Accademia a few years earlier to help compile a comprehensive history of the Redemptorists since their founding by St. Alphonsus

Liguori in 1732. He would soon become one of Murphy's most unlikely yet important contacts in Rome.

Sampers was a slight, bookish Italian who was far more comfortable in a room full of ancient manuscripts than a gathering of gregarious young seminarians and priests. He had a naively impish expression, offset by bushy eyebrows partially hidden behind wire rim glasses. His hair was dark, thick, and closely cropped. A strong nose and prominent forehead contrasted with long, slender, almost feminine fingers. In temperament he was the polar opposite of Murphy, who had become an immediate sensation among the clerics ensconced at the Accademia. And yet Sampers and Murphy established a wonderful rapport. Unlike most of the others, who tended to ignore Sampers, Murphy cajoled and teased him, but always in a polite and respectful way. For his part, Sampers looked at Murphy with gleeful curiosity, as an alter-ego that he never possessed – or really wanted – but nonetheless one that he was delighted to be associated with.

Sampers had a surprising breadth of professional contacts both within the Redemptorist order itself and throughout Rome in general and was proudly confidential. Murphy first came to this knowledge when, early upon his arrival in Rome, he had to deposit a number of checks, some quite substantial, that had been earned from various writing/journalistic assignments as well as from grateful families with newly adopted children back in the United States who continued to mail him regular updates on their families. These invariably included generous checks "to do with what you wish." Murphy's meager priestly pay had thus been supplemented well beyond what would have been considered appropriate by his Redemptorist superiors. Therefore, once he had cultivated a sufficient relationship with Sampers, Murphy asked for his assistance to quietly set up a separate, discrete account for this money. Sampers, at first reluctant, soon gave in to Murphy's charm and, in effect, became his covert personal banker.

Through Sampers, Murphy also renewed his acquaintance with another Italian priest, Monsignor Giovanni Benelli, whom he had briefly met in 1948 during his first assignment in Rome. Benelli was then the private secretary to the newly elevated Giovanni Cardinal Montini (eventual Paul VI). Murphy knew that Cardinal Montini, who had served for years in the Vatican Secretariat of State, had close relations with virtually every single Catholic powerbroker in Rome. Therefore, by developing a close relationship with Benelli, Murphy hoped to gain unique insider access. When Murphy learned that Benelli had an upcoming meeting with Sampers about some historical Vatican records housed at the Accademia, he asked if he could also attend. Never one to turn down an opportunity to impress his new American friend, Sampers complied. Benelli, just as Sampers, soon became enchanted with the gregarious American priest as well.

Benelli was affable, genial, warm-hearted to a fault. He was of medium build, somewhat lighter complexion, with a genuine smile that he readily proffered. He had a small mouth yet a disproportionately hearty laugh and subtle wrinkles around his eyes that portrayed sincere joy at every new introduction. He was loyal to a fault with his friends and colleagues, in particular to Cardinal Montini, whom he revered. However, contrary to his overall positive attitude toward most others, he vilified Montini's counterparts in the Vatican Curia, in particular Cardinal Ottaviani. He believed they were suffocating any progressive efforts that the Catholic Church could – and *should* – be undertaking in these tumultuous modern times. Murphy soon became well aware of, and would take full advantage of, Benelli's angrily emotional inclinations.

On January 25, 1959, Pope John summoned cardinals from dioceses throughout Italy as well as those serving in the Vatican Curia to the Basilica of St. Paul Outside the Walls, one of the four major basilicas of Rome and the second largest after St. Peter's. The location was not coincidental, signaling that this gathering was going to be of significance. With the grave of Saint Paul below the high altar under the magnificent Gothic marble baldachin created by Arnolfo di Cambio in 1285, and with the basilica's original incarnation pre-dating even St. Peter's itself, St. Paul Outside the Walls was a truly historic venue for Pope John to present his revolutionary idea for launching a global Ecumenical Council to the senior cardinals in Italy.

After celebrating Mass for the small and extremely elite gathering, Pope John slowly walked to the pulpit, looked down toward the expectant cardinals, and then beyond them and up toward the 267 *tondi* or circular paintings of each of his papal predecessors mounted along the walls of the extensive nave. Behind him was a huge fifth-century mosaic, originally commissioned by Pope Honorius III in 1220, depicting Christ teaching from an open book to his disciples. With this clearly symbolic backdrop, John began his talk with an overview of what he perceived to be the major issues currently facing the Catholic Church, expanding upon those he privately outlined a few weeks earlier to Cardinal Tardini: widespread societal unrest; a disaffected Catholic laity not engaged in the practice of their faith on a local level; the myopic, out-of-touch Vatican Curia; the need to make the College of Cardinals significantly larger and more globally diverse; and a revolutionary call for the healing of centuries-old divisions between the Catholic Church and other religions.

Pope John then dropped his bombshell. In order to fully understand and adequately address these and other issues so crucial to the future of the Church, he said it would be necessary to convene a full Ecumenical Council, calling to Rome religious leaders from throughout the world.

"I would now like to have your advice," he asked the gathered prelates.

To a man, the cardinals sat mute, staring, astonished.

Pope John waited. Silence. He slowly scanned his audience. There was not a word of encouragement, not even mild applause; their hardened sentiment was painfully obvious. He waited a full minute more. Still not a single response. In clear frustration and unfeigned disgust, he quickly said an awkward closing prayer, stepped down from the pulpit and abruptly left the basilica alone through a side door leading to the cloisters, leaving the stunned gathering of cardinals behind. As he was exiting, however, he could hear the agitated mutterings of his shocked religious colleagues.

Upon his return to the Vatican, John retreated to his private study and pulled out his personal diary. He wrote: "Humanly I could have expected that the cardinals, after hearing my address, might have crowded around to express approval and good wishes. Instead..." he paused, then continued writing, "...there was silence. Extraordinary SILENCE!!!"

A terrific pain suddenly shot through John's stomach and he doubled over onto the floor. In a few minutes, the pain subsided sufficiently for him to raise himself back up. He put down his pen and slowly, unsteadily, walked to the window with its commanding view of the dome of St. Peter's Basilica. He opened the window, inhaling deeply to calm himself. He then knelt in prayer at the sill – weakened, frustrated, physically and emotionally exhausted.

***

Although severely disappointed, Pope John was not naïve, especially regarding any expected pushback from the Curia. However, he was stunned at its virulence. Over the next two weeks a constant string of Curial cardinals requested individual audiences with the pontiff to express their deep concerns about the wisdom of holding such a global Council, its unattainable objectives, the overwhelming logistics that would be involved, and the unrealistic timeframe for staging such a massive undertaking within only a few short years. After listening serenely to entreaty after entreaty, John's determination to hold a Council became even more resolute. As each cardinal left and reported back to their frustrated colleagues on the continuing obstinance of the pope, a sense of disbelief, and then of panic, began to set in. Even Cardinal Ottaviani, who had purposefully been avoiding any close interactions with this pope, now requested a private audience.

"Holy Father," Cardinal Ottaviani began immediately after he sat down across the desk from Pope John. "So vast an undertaking as an Ecumenical Council will require many, many years of preparation."

Pope John smiled knowingly. This was a none-too-subtle allusion to his age and expected brief pontificate. And it was expected.

To soften his comment, Cardinal Ottaviani added, "I, of course, pray daily for your health, but I am worried that such an endeavor will…"

John raised his hand to interrupt. "Men are like wine, dear colleague. Some turn to vinegar," he said, looking directly at Cardinal Ottaviani, "but the best improve with age." In his own folksy way, Pope John could not have been more blunt. He was signaling in no uncertain terms that he was not backing down; in fact, just the opposite.

A long pause ensued. Pope John stared intently at Cardinal Ottaviani who, twice, began to speak but thought the better of it. Then, realizing that any further discussion would be futile, Ottaviani stood up, bowed almost imperceptibly, turned and walked slowly out of the papal office, clearly incensed. He went immediately to see Cardinal Tardini, whom he knew had become a close advisor to the pope. He bolted right through the anteroom of his office and entered without a knock.

"You are now the Secretary of State! The second-ranking member of the Church!" Ottaviani yelled in frustration. "Can you not talk sense into this pope?"

Tardini beckoned Ottaviani to sit down and collect himself. He then gave a nod for him to begin again. Ottaviani commenced with a lengthy diatribe on the reasons that such a colossal gathering of the entire Catholic Church leadership would be completely unthinkable in terms of logistics, the breadth of issues to be addressed, and – he mentioned not so delicately – the likelihood that this pope would not outlast his own delusions.

Tardini could not disagree with any of the points that Cardinal Ottaviani brought up, but in his heart he was loyal to Pope John. Then he suddenly conceived of a possible compromise. When he broached the idea to Cardinal Ottaviani, they both smiled in conspiratorial agreement.

The next morning, Cardinal Tardini asked for and received an immediate audience with the pope.

"And to your discussion with Cardinal Ottaviani?" Pope John asked without hesitation, as he had already anticipated such a follow-up meeting.

Tardini was taken aback but quickly composed himself.

"As you know," Tardini began, "Cardinal Ottaviani and, in truth, virtually all of the other members of the Curia, feel strongly that such an undertaking as an Ecumenical Council would be extremely challenging." He took a breath, then continued. "A Council may indeed have merits, but the details and the planning involved…" he paused, "that would have to be completely overseen by *them*," he emphasized with a nod in the direction of the Curial offices. "Well, they would be reluctant participants at best; if not, at the very least, significant roadblocks to any meaningful accomplishments."

Knowing that this would not dissuade Pope John, Tardini, ever the diplomat, offered his compromise. "What if you held a smaller Synod, an Ecumenical Council in miniature, if you will, for just the clergy here in Rome, to discuss local issues affecting only this archdiocese. It would at least give you a sense of the complexities involved."

Pope John understood that this was merely a delaying tactic on behalf of the Curial cardinals. But he was also disappointed that Cardinal Tardini, his supposedly trusted advisor, had been a party to it.

"It often happens that I dream at night about the serious problems facing our Church, our world, and decide I must tell the pope. Then I wake up in a cold sweat and remember that I *am* the pope," John said with a disheartened frown, "and that I have been entrusted with the keys of St. Peter, a sacred responsibility to act."

Although not sure why, Cardinal Tardini laughed uncomfortably at this comment. Nonetheless, the implications were clear. Pope John was ready to go it alone, if necessary, to pursue a full Ecumenical Council. The Curia, Tardini himself included, might have severely underestimated the resoluteness of this unassuming, aging pontiff.

Pope John thought for a moment, then suddenly brightened, perceiving an opening that he had not previously foreseen. Tardini was confused.

"If the Curia is willing to make efforts toward the preparation of a Synod just for Rome, then let us proceed," John said with an unexpected smile toward the bewildered cardinal.

"Immediately!" John then added with surprising enthusiasm.

<hr />

The two young priests, Father Murphy and Monsignor Benelli, had just finished a second round of scotches at the bar while waiting for a table at Murphy's favorite haunt, La Carbonara. The pasta was homemade and the wine and cocktail offerings moderately priced. Most important, however, the location was just far enough across the Tiber, sufficiently distant from the Vatican and its nearby restaurants and bars that were always over-populated with Curial bureaucrats. It was also comfortably noisy to ensure privacy in their conversations. Even the walls, completely covered with shelves of dusty wine bottles and fading prints of Roman landscapes, combined with the muted lighting throughout, somehow gave off an air of illicit collusion.

They were led through the crowded restaurant to a small table in a back corner by "our *bella ragazza*," as Father Murphy flirtatiously called their favorite waitress, Cristina. Over the past few months, Murphy, as a regular patron who often lingered well beyond a meal's completion, had gotten to know the earthy, naturally pretty, petite Italian brunette who was clearly fascinated with the brash American priest. She was likely in her early to mid-twenties (Murphy couldn't gauge well with Italian women), and she was confident in a very unassuming way. She had an alluring smile, especially toward Murphy, with dark, expressive eyes that lit up whenever he came into the restaurant, which was increasingly often. Her hair was always pulled back while at work. She wore minimal makeup; she didn't have to. She was usually dressed in a black pencil skirt with a fitted, button-down white top, both very flattering. A simple necklace with a silver cross and an occasional ring or two were the only jewelry she wore. Murphy and Cristina clearly enjoyed each other's company and, although her English was somewhat haphazard, it was easily counterbalanced by Murphy's own now-passing Italian.

Once seated by Cristina, and relatively reassured that the lively banter of their fellow diners would shield their own conversation, Murphy took no time in getting to the point.

"Well?" he immediately goaded Benelli, who was present with the newly-elevated Cardinal Montini at Pope John's audacious announcement regarding a proposed Council. "What happened at St. Paul Outside the Walls?"

Benelli, not even barely conflicted, began almost breathlessly, "A revolt. A revolt! The pope proposed a Council! Of all things! An Ecumenical Council!"

"I'll be *damned*," Murphy said in disbelief.

There was a long pause until Murphy prompted, "And...?"

"And nothing. Not a word was uttered by a single cardinal. Complete silence. The pope was stunned! And he just walked out!" Benelli blurted, sitting back to see Murphy's reaction.

"And...?" Murphy interjected again, impatiently.

Benelli leaned back in. "And since then, the cardinals in the Curia have been scheming against the pope. They actually came up with a plan to have a smaller local Synod in Rome instead, to show the pope how much work would be involved in even *that* type of gathering."

"Heh, heh...to basically wait him out," responded Murphy, acknowledging the cardinals' cleverness. "Doing the math with his age."

"Exactly."

There was another pause while Murphy waited again for Benelli to continue.

"And…?" Murphy finally blurted.

"They had old Cardinal Tardini present the idea to Pope John, figuring that he was the closest to him and therefore the one John would most likely listen to."

After another maddeningly long pause, waiting for Benelli to continue, Murphy growled, "Aaaaand…?"

Benelli, clearly enjoying having Murphy's rapt attention, continued, "Well, Tardini reported back to the cardinals that the pope was indeed open to a much smaller local Synod in Rome. And yet…" He sat back again in his chair, looking around, somewhat conflicted about continuing.

Murphy didn't give him a chance. "Dear God, Benelli. WHAT?"

"And yet, according to Cardinal Tardini, John somehow seemed even more committed to a full Ecumenical Council than ever. It just doesn't make sense…"

"Damn," Murphy said, intrigued.

"I feel for Tardini," lamented Benelli. "All he wanted to do was retire so he could devote his final days to the Villa Nazareth orphanage. Now he's caught up in all of this Vatican infighting. He's not healthy to begin with and this stress could kill him."

Murphy looked away, pondering, then refocused on Benelli.

"Could you get me an introduction? To meet Cardinal Tardini?" Murphy finally asked. He had met him briefly years earlier during his first stint in Rome but was certain Tardini would not remember him.

Benelli looked quizzically at Murphy, uncertain of his intentions. Nonetheless, he relented, ready to please his new American friend. "I think I can. I'll let you know."

Pope John set to work earnestly, knowing full well that the circle of those whom he could truly trust was now extremely small. And that it apparently did *not* include his Secretary of State, Cardinal Tardini, whom he now knew was susceptible to the power plays of the scheming Curial cardinals. However, there was one person he could indeed trust, with *absolute* certainty, and that was his personal secretary, Father Loris Capovilla.

Short and wiry, with a pointy nose, chiseled face, and well-defined chin, Capovilla gave off a no-nonsense air, softened somewhat by slightly-too-large ears and spectacles that seemed a bit thicker than necessary. He walked with fast determination and his posture was always erect – a dramatic physical counterpoint to his lumbering boss whenever he and the pope were observed walking together. Capovilla had a reputation for both extreme loyalty and complete discretion.

The pope, back when he was the newly installed Cardinal Roncalli in Venice, first met Capovilla in 1953. Capovilla had already established a name for himself as a talented priest/journalist with a knack for public affairs.

On that basis alone, he was more than qualified to be the personal secretary to the new cardinal. However, what impressed Roncalli most was a story that he had heard about Capovilla's wartime service. In 1943, when Italy had just surrendered to the Allies, Nazi Germany still had troops stationed throughout much of the rural Italian countryside. This included an air base in Parma where ten pilots of the Italian Air Force were being held captive. Capovilla, a young Italian military chaplain at the base, overheard plans for the imminent deportation of the pilots to a prison camp inside Germany. Extremely slight in stature, Capovilla managed to convince the German guards that he needed help from some of the pilots to move heavy furniture in his office. Then, riding his bike back and forth from the prisoner barracks to his office followed by two similarly dressed but different pilots on every trip, he was somehow able to quietly spirit all ten of them away to a partisan escape route just before the Nazis abandoned the base in anticipation of the pending Allied advance. Before his ploy was discovered, he was lucky to make his own way to safety amidst the chaotic German retreat.

It was a remarkable tale that reminded Roncalli of his own ruse with forged baptismal certificates to save Jews in Turkey during the war. They therefore had a mutual appreciation for creative thinking and, when necessary, a bit of collusion and sleight-of-hand that would prove invaluable in the contentious months leading up to what would soon become Vatican Council II.

The two men hatched a plan.

"Let's give them what they want!" Pope John chortled with a sly grin to Capovilla. "Send them in."

When Cardinals Ottaviani and Tardini entered, Pope John came around his desk and extended to both an overly hearty handshake, bypassing the traditional papal greeting. "Please, please sit down," he offered warmly and they took their seats. Their expressions were severe, wary.

"Let me begin by telling you that it has been an interesting start to this papacy," the pope began. "Indeed, *quite* interesting." He gazed intently at the pair, who were uncertain as to the underlying meaning of his comment, not to mention why they were being summoned in the first place. "In response to my idea for an Ecumenical Council, you have suggested that I am completely naïve as to the complexities that would be involved in such an undertaking." Ottaviani and Tardini looked quizzically at each other, then nodded simultaneously in agreement, wondering if the pope had finally come to his senses. John continued, "You have further suggested that a smaller local Synod for the clergy here in the Archdiocese of Rome would provide just such a realistic understanding. Am I correct?"

Tardini looked carefully at Ottaviani, then spoke up first. "Holy Father, since you are also the Patriarch of the Archdiocese of Rome," he began, "such a Synod would be a welcome gesture to your local flock."

"I agree," said Pope John. "My thought exactly. Let us hold this Synod, without delay, within the next 6 months."

Both cardinals looked at each other, not certain who should respond. Ottaviani finally spoke up. "Holy Father, the preparations for such a Synod could take years," he shot back, not even trying to conceal his frustration.

"I disagree," John responded. "Could not the direct involvement of the Curia in the planning of this Synod help to expedite the effort?"

Seizing on what he saw as a remarkable opportunity, and not wanting it to slip away, Ottaviani responded immediately. "Of course, Holy Father. I would be honored to personally oversee the preparations for the Synod if you wish."

As Ottaviani well knew, any documents promulgated by this local Synod, all of which he would ensure had an overwhelmingly conservative imprint, would be published in *L'Osservatore Romano*, the official Vatican newspaper. It would enable Ottaviani to propagate his ultra-orthodox ideologies to clergy around the world – with a Vatican blessing no less! He smiled toward whom he considered a remarkably naïve pope.

"Well then, we are all in complete agreement?" asked Pope John, a bit too readily thought both Tardini and Ottaviani, suddenly cautious.

"Yes, Holy Father," they each responded, but with a bit of vigilance. They looked quizzically at each other.

As Pope John came around his desk to dismiss them, they noticed that he seemed...jaunty? Clearly out of character for any pontiff, let alone this generally subdued one. Maybe it was a sign of relief, they thought, an acknowledgement that he finally understood that holding even a small, local Synod in Rome was a laudable accomplishment in itself for his almost certainly brief papacy.

It was a sign indeed.

As they were exiting the office, Cardinal Ottaviani looked back and noticed Pope John turning toward his open window overlooking the piazza, a broad smile clearly evident on his face.

———◆———

A few minutes after Cardinals Ottaviani and Tardini left, the Vatican physician came into Pope John's office with difficult news, not wholly unexpected.

"It is not an ulcer, Holy Father," he said in a grievous tone. There was a pause as the physician tried to collect himself. He took a deep breath. "It is cancer of the stomach." He paused again and bowed his head. "I am so very sorry."

"If it *was* an ulcer," John responded, "I would know *exactly* who to blame!" he scowled half-heartedly, then smiled, wanly, gently.

"Your treatment…" the physician resumed hesitantly, but John interjected.

"Two of my sisters died of cancer. I will finally be able to empathize with their suffering," John said with melancholy. He closed his eyes, reflecting back.

After a few moments, the physician began again. "There are…" but John raised his hand.

"No, no. Just medicine to help ease the pain. That is all. It is God's will."

"But…"

"And most important of all, this must remain between just the two of us."

"You have my word, Holy Father. You have my word."

"I trust you. And that is good because, if not, I have my *ways*," Pope John said with a wink. The physician grimaced uncertainly. "Relax, my friend," John said to ease his angst. "As my father used to say, 'Never distress the cow that supplies your milk.'"

Father Murphy and Monsignor Benelli had begun to form a close friendship. While Murphy spoke passing Italian, although remarkably well given his limited time in Italy, Benelli spoke near-fluent English with a beautiful sing-song lilt. Murphy, a newcomer to Rome and Vatican politics, was still a complete outsider. Benelli, on the other hand, was a true insider, having served for over a decade as a lower-level bureaucrat in the Vatican diplomatic corps prior to becoming Cardinal Montini's personal secretary. It was this tenure that forever blackened Benelli's views of the Curia and its intrigues.

"Ottaviani has him where he wants him," Benelli whispered as soon as they were seated by Cristina at a back corner table at La Carbonara. A wink by Murphy and she was off to bring them their scotches.

"Both Ottaviani and Tardini met with Pope John the other day and finally convinced him that an Ecumenical Council was out of the question," Benelli said. He then glanced around before continuing in a low tone. "Apparently Pope John saw the light and reluctantly agreed to their idea of a smaller Synod – for just the clergy in Rome." Benelli lowered his head to the center of the table. Murphy followed his lead. "Ottaviani is determined to control the entire Synod. He offered to craft all of the preliminary survey questions to be asked of the Roman priests and bishops, have the Holy Office collate the results, then personally draft the final report."

"And Pope John agreed to this?" queried Murphy in disbelief.

"What could he do?" muttered Benelli. "He had no choice. He's too new and too old to go it alone." Murphy laughed at this clever wordplay in English, which pleased Benelli tremendously. Benelli continued. "The best part, according to Ottaviani, is that the end result will be a report with detailed requirements for the clergy in Rome on how to conduct the day-to-day practice of their offices – in the centuries-old, traditional manner. And, once it's finalized it will be published in *L'Osservatore Romano* and disseminated all over the world – with the pope's imprimatur no less!"

"Brilliant, I must say. Absolutely brilliant!" responded Murphy. "And Ottaviani can drag things out as long as he wants, ensuring that the idea for a full Ecumenical Council dies with this pope. In the worst case, if this Synod does indeed come to fruition, Ottaviani has a global pulpit for his personal agenda, gift-wrapped by Pope John!"

"Exactly," said Benelli, proud to have impressed Murphy with the gossip.

"Ottaviani *is* a bastard," Murphy continued. "A devious bastard…but a clever one." He paused. "Who else knows about this?"

"It's an open secret within the Curia. They're all on board with Ottaviani, of course. Beyond that, not many. They're going to get away with it."

As Cristina approached, they both sat back in their chairs, smiling at her as she delivered their drinks. When she left, Murphy muttered connivingly to Benelli, "We'll see."

Over the next few months, throughout the spring and summer of 1959, Cardinal Ottaviani and his second-in-command in the Holy Office, Archbishop Pietro Parente, mailed surveys to hundreds of clerics within the Archdiocese of Rome to identify those issues they viewed as the most important to fulfilling their pastoral duties. Parente was the perfect complement to Ottaviani in the Holy Office. He was ruthlessly loyal to both the cardinal and to the extremely conservative religious worldview that he espoused. Parente was a compact, powerfully built man of few words. He was intimidating, a reputation he relished. He had a strong, thick neck that conveyed strength and determination. His eyes were intense; he rarely smiled. He would have been well suited in the ancient Office of the Inquisition, a thought that he privately relished. The Catholic Church, he believed, was meant to be an anchor against contemporary, short-lived trends, and he was determined to protect that historic role.

As the multitude of responses were received by the Holy Office, they were rapidly collated, analyzed, and summarized by a hand-picked clique of Cardinal Ottaviani's trusted staff. Periodically, the cardinal briefed Pope John on the essence of the emerging findings. What was shocking was not the ultra-orthodox skew of the Ottaviani-edited compilations but rather that Pope John was not questioning how the Holy Office had come to its conclusions. Furthermore, the pope had initially envisioned the Synod as a series of open-ended discussions with the clergy of Rome. However, Cardinal Ottaviani argued that the only way to make the pope's ambitious deadline was for the Holy Office alone to analyze the survey findings and then issue a final report to the Synod. Once again, Pope John surprisingly gave his assent.

The late-night phone call and mysterious invitation to visit Cardinal Tardini were completely unexpected by Father Murphy.

The next morning, he found himself standing with the cardinal in front of a formidable, two-story, somewhat decrepit brownish-red brick building, with only a single forlorn tree breaking up the expanse of dirt fronting the Villa Nazareth orphanage. About a dozen oversized arched windows covered most of the left front façade, with a small, carefully-tended chapel adjoining the right. There was an eerie lack of sound; Murphy would have expected a cacophony of noise from an orphanage full of boys and girls.

"Well, this is Villa Nazareth, my friend," said Tardini to Murphy, who gazed forward, taking it all in. "I founded it after the war to help orphaned boys and girls get an education, to get the tools to help them survive as adults." He paused, scanning from left to right. "It has not gone well. After so many years, there are still too many unwanted children and we have to turn many others away."

Murphy did not respond, still uncertain why Cardinal Tardini had invited him here, although it was likely related to his earlier request to Monsignor Benelli for an introduction. They slowly made their way toward a heavy, well-aged wooden front door. Behind it they heard the faint sing-song murmurs of children reciting rote catechisms after prompts from female voices. "Those are the Sisters of Charity," said Tardini. "Selfless, hardworking, true saints on this earth."

Tardini raised and lowered a large, brass knocker, but with no response he simply opened the door with an obvious familiarity. Inside, the orphanage was welcomingly cool compared to the oppressive heat outside. Murphy now noted the reason for the large windows, which invited natural light into an expansive, high-ceilinged lobby. They walked through the lobby to an interior, open plot of haphazard grass and dirt, which was surrounded on all sides by two levels of what looked like dormitory rooms, none with doors. Dozens of children were seated on the ground in neat rows in front of a trio of nuns, two older, one noticeably younger. A stiff coif framed each of the nuns' faces, a long white wimple extending up under their chins and down onto their chests, upon which were simple wooden crosses that rested unevenly against the heavily starched linen. The children themselves ranged in age from three or four up to their early teens. They were clothed in variations of gray shorts and buttonless shirts, virtually all were shoeless. They seemed uniformly clean though, as were their clothes, which were nonetheless careworn and extensively hemmed. All of them were thin, but not alarmingly so.

One of the older nuns, apparently the Mother Superior, glanced subtly over at Cardinal Tardini, nodded knowingly, then focused back on her task of shepherding the children through their psalmist repetitions.

"When you requested to meet me here, I was surprised," Murphy finally said to Tardini.

Neither looked at each other but kept their focus on the children and nuns in front of them.

"Your reputation precedes you," responded Tardini.

Not sure what to make of this, Murphy let it linger, watching intently as the children continued with their lesson.

"I found it noteworthy that you spent time in Germany, is that so?" queried Tardini.

"Yes, during the Korean War, Your Eminence," acknowledged Murphy.

"And did you witness the same plight of children without parents?"

Murphy hesitated. "Well, yes and no," he said guardedly, unsure what direction this inquiry was going to take and somewhat offended at Tardini's knowledge of his past activities. "There were mothers with children abandoned by American soldiers. They were unable to care for them and…"

"And here," Tardini interrupted, "we have the same. The stigma toward unwed mothers after the war as well as during the economic collapse since…so many abandoning their children." He paused. "The guilt. The innocent children."

Murphy waited, now knowing where this was going.

"Father, may I ask, did you help orphaned children in Germany find homes in America?" Tardini queried.

"Your Eminence," Murphy responded hesitantly, "I… um…well…yes."

"Here in Italy, it is often very difficult to work with the government and social services, each with their own agendas," Tardini continued. "Our cause is sincere, the need is so great, yet it is often a challenge to overcome unnecessary obstacles." He now looked directly at Murphy. "Do you understand my dilemma?"

Murphy, still looking straight ahead, unwittingly nodded.

"My dear Father Murphy, I am an old man, my health is failing, and yet my true vocation remains unresolved."

Murphy waited for the cardinal to elaborate, but he did not. Tardini simply nodded to the Mother Superior, who seemed to understand his gesture of goodbye, then he took Murphy by the arm and led him back outside. Once there he turned to Murphy and said, "I have someone I want you to meet."

<hr />

A few days prior to the start of the Synod in Rome, which was now set for January 24, 1960, Cardinal Ottaviani scheduled a meeting with Pope John to review the final draft of the proposed Synodal Acts, diligently culled from the hundreds of surveys of Italian priests that had been evaluated and summarized by the Holy Office. Not surprisingly, at least to John, it had only taken a matter of weeks to complete. The proposed Acts covered an excruciatingly detailed and oppressively wide range of topics controlling the daily lives of the Roman clergy. For example, they specified in detail how priests should act if their honor was attacked in public; the respect they should show to policemen; the timeliness of their payments for traffic violations; how they should interpret financial and tax laws; and even how many times they should visit cemeteries each year. The proposed Acts went so far as to mandate that all priests in Rome should shave the back tops of their heads in the ancient "tonsure" to emphasize their vocation. They even called for a prohibition of priests attending "public spectacles" of any kind, from operas to horse races.

Throughout Cardinal Ottaviani's lengthy reading of the proposed requirements, Pope John's mind often seemed elsewhere, with a small grin sometimes flitting its way across his face. Once Ottaviani finished, he sat back in his chair with smug self-satisfaction. Then, worried that the pope might not be able to fully grasp, let alone convey, the many details of the Acts, he graciously offered to present them personally to the Synodal convocation.

"Thank you, my dear cardinal," Pope John replied, with barely feigned sincerity. "But as the Patriarch of Rome, it is my duty." And with a pause and a very subtle curl of his lips, he added, "And I will of course give credit where credit is due."

In a speech at the majestic Basilica of St. John Lateran, with hundreds of clerics from Rome in attendance, Pope John dutifully presented the findings compiled by Cardinal Ottaviani and his staff of the Holy Office, giving them complete and total credit in the most magnanimous way. The venue of St. John Lateran had been personally chosen by Cardinal Ottaviani. It was founded in 324 and was the oldest basilica in the Western World. What better setting, Ottaviani thought, to reinforce the importance of adhering to the Church's ancient tenets regulating the day-to-day behavior of its priests.

To a man, the gathered clerics were outraged when they heard the proposed new requirements, although they held their indignation in check until the pope concluded his summation and took his leave from the basilica. Immediately thereafter, however, a tempest of anger was unleashed, all of it directed toward Cardinal Ottaviani and the Holy Office rather than at their beloved but apparently duped pontiff.

The promulgated Acts were duly published in the *L'Osservatore Romano* with full credit once again being given to the Holy Office under the leadership of Cardinal Ottaviani. The Acts were thus widely disseminated to Catholic clergy around the world. While initially thrilled at the promulgation of his orthodox ideology, Ottaviani and his colleagues were soon astonished by the immediacy, the intensity, and the vitriol of the global outcry against it.

It was not surprising to Pope John, however. In fact, it was exactly what he had intended.

"I am *not* shaving my head!" Father Murphy declared loudly, pounding his fist on the table when he read a summary of the Synod of Rome's declarations published in the *International Herald Tribune*. He was sitting in a bustling outdoor café, Ricci Salumiere, on the Piazza della Rotonda in the shadow of the Pantheon. He had just been joined by a literary agent from New York, John Chapin, who happened to be in Rome on vacation. Murphy had met Chapin at a formal reception at the American Embassy the previous night and, over numerous cocktails, learned of Chapin's publishing background and extensive network of literary contacts. Murphy had asked to have lunch with Chapin the following day.

"Cardinal Ottaviani has his head up his ass!" blurted Murphy, although when he looked up from the newspaper he apologized and corrected himself sheepishly "…in the sand."

"What do you mean?" inquired a slightly shocked but clearly intrigued Chapin. "And who is Cardinal Ottaviani?"

"Would you be interested in a story, John? About what *really* goes on behind the walls of the Vatican?"

"Indeed I might," responded Chapin. "Let's keep in touch."

***

With the Synod of Rome, Cardinal Ottaviani had unwittingly demonstrated to Pope John that a large number of Catholic clergy could be efficiently surveyed and their responses collated in a timely manner. Furthermore, the hail of global protest following publication of the Synodal Acts also proved to Pope John beyond any doubt that there was a remarkable gulf of opinion between the insulated, myopic, ultra-conservative Curia and the real life beliefs and practices of priests and religious in Rome… and presumably throughout the world.

Pope John's response to the post-Synodal dissent? A separate published expression of gratitude in *L'Osservatore Romano* to Cardinal Ottaviani and the Holy Office for their diligent efforts, which he would take "under advisement." But no papal edict on the Synod would be forthcoming in the foreseeable future or, it turned out, ever.

Cardinal Tardini soon realized the deftness of the pope's Synodal strategy as a cagey steppingstone to launching a full Ecumenical Council; and, quite frankly, he was impressed. The pope had used Cardinal Ottaviani to not only demonstrate on a small scale the feasibility of calling forth a full Ecumenical Council but he had also used Ottaviani's own ego against him. "A brilliant gambit," Tardini muttered to himself, smiling.

Cardinal Ottaviani had grudgingly come to the same conclusion.

CHAPTER IV

"The smallest of windows can shed light on the greatest of truths."

Pope John immediately set to work, relying heavily on both his personal secretary, Father Capovilla, and the newly chastened Cardinal Tardini, under whose purview the upcoming Ecumenical Council would fall, as well as a small but trustworthy cadre of priests, theologians, and lay people. However, the scope of the proposed Council soon became alarmingly evident, and it was staggering. It meant the surveying of every single one of the Catholic Church's 2,500 cardinals and bishops, the heads of all religious orders, and the faculties of the Catholic universities scattered throughout the world. Pope John's incredibly ambitious objective was to ascertain, in a candid, unfiltered way, what these religious leaders collectively viewed as the most important problems facing the Catholic Church – both internally regarding the day-to-day practice of the faith and externally in relation to the Church's role in modern society.

───────◆───────

Over the next few months, and over the increasingly vehement protests of virtually all of the cardinals in the Curia, most notably the still-seething Cardinal Ottaviani, a remarkably comprehensive, open-ended questionnaire was unilaterally crafted by Pope John's inner circle. At John's firm behest, it placed absolutely no limitations on the issues that could be considered and debated during what was now being officially called Vatican Council II.

Thousands of detailed surveys were mailed all over the world in the course of a single week, a massive undertaking for the traditionally plodding Vatican Post Office – and one that necessitated more than a few special trips of encouragement and gratitude by the pontiff himself. Within the next two months, close to two thousand responses were received by the Vatican. The pope had made it clear from the start that he wanted to hear the authentic, unfiltered viewpoints of the entire Church leadership, and he was not disappointed. Feedback ranged from the practical (having daily Mass said in local languages, forgiveness for divorced Catholics, allowing concelebration of the Mass by multiple priests, etc.), to extremely ambitious (reuniting all Christian denominations, official apologies for historic Church transgressions, etc.), to even debating the source of divine

Revelation itself. The stakes for the future of the Roman Catholic Church were enormous.

To handle such an expansive trove of material, it was necessary to create a number of Preparatory Commissions, new bodies established by the pope to review and categorize all of the incoming responses. These commissions would then be responsible for developing schema (frameworks for debate) to guide all of the discussions of the Council. The cardinals in the Curia, once they realized that Vatican Council II was inevitable, pressured Pope John to place *them* in charge of these Preparatory Commissions, arguing that *only they* had the expertise to efficiently coordinate such a wealth of information. Pope John reluctantly agreed, given the enormous scope of the enterprise, but he countered their ploy by creating a brand new, overarching Central Preparatory Commission that would have final authority on all matters related to the Council. He placed himself as its president.

The cardinals in the Curia wasted no time in quickly saturating the Preparatory Commissions with trusted staff, i.e., conservative colleagues. And, as Cardinal Ottaviani unabashedly cautioned, so what if the preliminary work of the Preparatory Commissions took much longer than Pope John anticipated? With so many topics to be processed and evaluated – many contentious, some extremely volatile – who knew when they would finally complete their work? It could take years.

However, Pope John did not have years. His pain was becoming more chronic and acute. His meetings and audiences were necessarily shorter; his demeanor more serious; his mood less jovial; his anger toward the Curia more intensified.

"There is a time to every purpose under heaven," he told Father Capovilla, paraphrasing from Ecclesiastes, "and it is NOT dictated by the Roman Curia!"

***

There were ten advance Preparatory Commissions that began their work over the next nine months. However, from the outset it became evident that their draft schema would primarily reflect the Curia's narrow ultra-conservative viewpoints rather than objectively incorporating the broad range of ideas that had actually been submitted by prelates from around the world.

The most notoriously biased of the schema were those processed by the Preparatory Theological Commission, headed by Cardinal Ottaviani and stacked with his cohorts from the Congregation of the Holy Office, most notably its chief inquisitor, Archbishop Parente. With an especially broad mandate, engineered cleverly at the outset by Cardinal Ottaviani himself, the Preparatory Theological Commission had influence in shaping virtually every important debate that would take place during the Council. Although Cardinal Ottaviani had not been successful in preventing Vatican Council II from convening in the first place, he was determined to at least control the scope of the deliberations and eventual outcomes (if any) from its proceedings.

In the end, a failure of Vatican II – and thus, in his view, avoiding its potentially cataclysmic reforms – would be a victory for the status quo that he and his Curial colleagues desperately sought to preserve.

<hr>

Father Murphy walked with trepidation, unusual for him, to the luxurious Hotel Majestic, the Roman landmark on Via Veneto favored by Italian glitterati since the turn of the century. He entered through the ornate lobby and ascended to the intimate and secluded terrace café with its softly candle-lit, white-linen covered tables. At a far corner was seated possibly the most elegant Italian woman he had ever seen. Cardinal Tardini had playfully referred to her as "La Princesa" but his brief description was clearly inadequate. She saw Murphy enter, smiled, then casually beckoned him over to her table. As he approached, he couldn't help but notice her auburn, perfectly coiffed hair, dark eyes, soft complexion, and long, tanned legs crossed to the side of the table and purposefully in view. She had a striking natural beauty, highlighted with a tasteful amount of makeup, and full red lips. She wore a flowing silk floral print dress with a plunging neckline, which was especially apparent when she remained seated as Murphy approached. His gaze lingered just a bit too long, which she noticed. He took in a wisp of her perfume. She might have been in her early forties or late thirties. He didn't dwell on her age. She was simply stunning.

She raised her hand, Murphy kissed it, then he sat down across the table from her.

"Come sit next to me," she ordered politely, in well-spoken but heavily accented English. "That way we can talk more privately."

"As you wish," Murphy responded without hesitation as he shifted to the closer seat.

"My name is Luciana. I am a very close friend of dear Cardinal Tardini," she began with an affected whisper. "And I hope he spoke well of me."

"Indeed he did not do you justice," Murphy remarked, somewhat awkwardly, regretting immediately that he was focusing solely on her beauty with his comment.

She noticed. "Thank you."

Murphy was uncomfortable in the ensuing silence. She was not.

"Please call me Frank," he finally interjected. She smiled and nodded, as if that was to be expected. She was clearly comfortable in these surroundings, as she likely would be in any situation in which she found herself. There was an air of confidence about her, a calming presence, and it now put Murphy at ease.

"May I ask why Cardinal Tardini wanted me to make your acquaintance?" he asked.

She put a finger to his lips. "Let us simply enjoy a meal together, Frank," she whispered softly, "then we can talk of other things. And I want you to call me Luciana, please."

Toward the end of a truly exquisite dinner, Murphy realized that he had droned on even more than usual. And yet Luciana had seemed politely rapt throughout, peppering him with casual questions about his family and friends, his travels, his first impressions of Rome. Subtly, however, over the course of the meal, her queries became more probing: his time spent in Germany, the closeness of his contacts within the Vatican, his feelings toward the upcoming Vatican Council, his passions and personal pleasures. Unassumingly, and in a remarkably brief period of time, she had gotten to know more about Murphy than possibly anyone else in Rome. And with deep regret, he realized that he had passed up an opportunity to learn virtually anything of even minimal importance about his beautiful dinner companion. She was clearly very adept at steering conversations to her designated ends while protecting her own privacy.

Finally, as the remnants of panna cotta were cleared, Murphy moved the conversation back to her.

"Luciana, may I ask about your relationship with Cardinal Tardini?" he said hesitatingly.

"Of course," she assented, lighting a cigarette, shifting back casually in her seat and re-crossing her legs.

Murphy, somewhat uncomfortably, followed up. "And what would that be?"

She looked at him directly. "Well, my dear Frank...you see...I have a son."

He inhaled perceptibly, seemingly disappointed by this comment. She noticed.

"There is no father," she continued.

With a bit of too-forced empathy, Murphy responded, "I'm sorry. May I ask…"

She quickly interrupted, "I was given the blessed gift of my son, Fabrizio, through the good graces of Cardinal Tardini."

Ahh, Murphy thought to himself, finally putting the connection with the cardinal's orphanage together.

"And it was not an easy process," she continued. "So very difficult and no rational reason for why we had such challenges." She leaned into Murphy. He responded in kind. "You see," she said softly, lowering her voice, "sometimes here in Italy one must use imaginative ways to fulfill one's desires." She smiled teasingly at him, observing his uncertainty about how to react to her innuendo, then added, "And from what I have heard, you understand this too, no?" She leaned in even closer.

Murphy was clearly *not* sure how to respond. He simply nodded his head.

"There were so many orphans here in Italy at the end of the war – and so many more in the decades since. So few options for them with our broken economy, our politics, our stigmas." She paused and sighed. "It continues to this day."

Murphy sat silently, listening intently.

"America is such a big country, a welcoming country," she went on, still in a whisper. Murphy leaned in closer. "I

know my Italy. I know how things must be done here…
sometimes in unconventional ways. And I am indebted to
dear Cardinal Tardini for his invaluable knowledge of that
process. I have supported his beloved Villa Nazareth very
generously ever since. But there are possibly other ways
that I…we…might now have to explore."

It was Murphy's turn to pause, comprehending the
unequivocal "we." She waited. He relented. "I am of course
willing to help in any way that I can," he said, without quite
thinking through the implications of his response.

Luciana smiled and sat back in her chair. Murphy followed her lead, both letting the furtive moment sink in.
Murphy had thought this dinner might be a possible first
step inside the hierarchical sphere of Cardinal Tardini and
his secretive dealings within the Vatican Curia; however, it
now looked like the price for that quid pro quo was going
to be a bit more complicated. And yet, as he sat there in
that remarkable setting with this fascinating, mysterious
woman, it was clearly a path that he was more than willing
to consider.

**A week later Murphy received a call in the middle of
the night**. He was startled awake by the halting voice of
Luciana apologizing and asking if this was a good time to
speak with him. He was immediately alert and overly effusive in his response.

"Of course it is. Any time you call it will be a pleasure."

He waited for a similarly demonstrative reply but none was forthcoming. Instead there was lingering silence on the other line. He continued to wait.

"Hello?" he said after a few moments.

He heard faint sniffling. "Luciana?" he said. "Luciana?"

"Cardinal Tardini has passed," she said finally, clearly upset.

"What? How?"

"A heart attack. He has left us, left this world," she uttered amid sobs.

"I am so very sorry," Murphy responded with sincere empathy. "I did not know him until very recently."

"Can we get together soon, Frank?" she asked. "I must see you."

"Of course," he responded.

"We have much work to do. And now, without the dear Cardinal, we…" She did not finish her sentence.

With that she hung up. Again the "we." Murphy lay awake that night, confused. Delighted?

———◆———

On August 2, 1961, Pope John presided at the solemn requiem Mass in St. Peter's Basilica for Domenico Cardinal Tardini, referring to him as one of his closest friends and most trusted advisors. Following the ancient rites for burying a cardinal of the Church, and witnessed by not only the Vatican ecclesiastical elite but also ambassadors from around the world because of his station as Secretary of State, the huge basilica was crowded to overflowing. Murphy was there at the special invitation and as the escort of Luciana, who was dressed in classic, form-fitting black. Throughout the hours-long service she held his hand, hardly keeping her emotions in check, but without a word being said. Afterward, they walked a few blocks, her arm interlocked within his, to get distance from the massive public crowds that had assembled in St. Peter's Square to pay their own respects. Soon a car slowly approached and stopped next to them. The driver got out and opened the door; Luciana slid in and beckoned Murphy to follow. They drove a few miles to the spacious Piazza Navona with Bernini's spectacular Fountain of the Four Rivers encircled by teeming outdoor cafes. They exited the car and the driver pointed to a quaint restaurant, La Piccola Cuccagna, tucked into a small side street just distant enough from the bustling crowds in the piazza. They found a table toward the rear, and Luciana ordered two espressos – not cocktails, not even lunch, as Murphy had anticipated.

"I am tired, my dear Frank. I have not much slept in the past few days. Please forgive me," she said haltingly.

"There is nothing to forgive," Murphy responded with sincerity.

"I will be forever indebted to Cardinal Tardini," she began. "I have my beloved son to thank him for, a truly miraculous blessing."

"Was he indeed an orphan at Villa Nazareth?" inquired Murphy, suddenly feeling more comfortable with direct questioning.

"Yes. One of far too many. He has filled a deep void in my life, one caused for many reasons."

Murphy waited for her to elaborate but she did not.

"There were so many other children there, none with a family, all desperately seeking one. It was such a joyous day for me when I first met my son, but also heart-breaking. In the months that followed, the policies of the bureaucrats – the selfish, ignorant, dirty bureaucrats – almost destroyed it all. They wanted papers that did not exist. They wanted money, so much money, much of it going who knows where. And then the charitable organizations, with their own demands, wanting even more money, wanting credit for their work. It was a nightmare but, with the help and influence of Cardinal Tardini and my own financial resources, we finally prevailed."

For the first time, Murphy could see anger in Luciana, something she was unsuccessfully trying to keep at bay.

"We learned how... how do you Americans say it? To 'work the system' – and we took similar approaches to place about a dozen other children with families throughout Rome." She paused, picking up a napkin, dabbing the corner of her eye. "However, Cardinal Tardini's influence, his leverage, his protection, is no longer there."

Murphy now realized that he was suddenly becoming involved in much more than he had originally foreseen.

"Before he passed," Luciana continued, "Cardinal Tardini told me about your efforts to place orphan children from Germany with families in America. Is this true?"

Hesitantly, Murphy nodded his head.

They both waited, Murphy not wanting to offer too much and Luciana reluctant to ask an extremely presumptuous next question they both knew was forthcoming.

A lingering minute passed, uncomfortably.

"Cardinal Tardini had a dream that I must now help to fulfill," she said. "I owe him a debt of gratitude that I will never be able to repay…but I must try." She looked directly, intensely, at Murphy. "I must ask if you will help me."

There was no flirtation in that statement. Rather, it came across as powerful, resonant.

"I am in a financial position to still facilitate many things here in Rome, but it will not be possible to sidestep the Church and place orphan children with families in Italy without Cardinal Tardini's influence. Therefore, we must look elsewhere."

Murphy once again took notice of the pronoun "we."

"Will you help me, Frank?" she repeated again. Her gaze was firm. It was a different side to her, well-hidden but intense.

"How?" Murphy responded hesitatingly.

That was the opening Luciana had been hoping for. "Can I assume that you still have friends in America who might help place some of these children?" she asked.

Murphy, both cautious yet oddly flattered, nodded yes.

"Could I prevail upon you to contact some of them on our behalf?" She caught herself and corrected, "On behalf of these desperate children?" She realized early on that Murphy had that famous male American ego, one that she felt certain she could manipulate. She was not naïve in understanding that Murphy's original objective was to take advantage of Cardinal Tardini's high-level Vatican access for his own purposes. But she also knew that Murphy was intrigued by her, on many levels, something she knew full well how to exploit.

"Yes, I will help you, Luciana," Murphy responded, far quicker than she had anticipated. She smiled broadly, reached over and, to his surprise, kissed him gently on the lips. Then she sat back in her seat, looking directly into his eyes. "I am so, so very happy, my dear new friend."

***

Months passed and the cardinals in charge of the various Preparatory Commissions continued to complain bitterly about their "monumental" task of sifting through, categorizing, analyzing, and then summarizing all of the information that had been submitted in response to Pope John's global survey. When finally confronted by the pope, who was alarmed at the minimal progress of their efforts, Cardinal Ottaviani, speaking on behalf of his supposedly beleaguered colleagues, cautioned of their need to be "extremely deliberate" for such an historic undertaking. He warned that the process would likely take much, *much* longer than originally planned.

Just as worrisome to Pope John was that all of the work of the various Preparatory Commissions was being conducted behind closed doors "to protect the integrity of the process," as Cardinal Ottaviani self-servingly proclaimed. Pope John anticipated that there would likely be a conservative skew to their eventual schema for guiding the discussions, something he felt he was well prepared to counterbalance once the full Council convened, but he at least needed their preparatory work to be near completion before he could set an official date for the opening of Vatican Council II.

Finally, though, he had waited long enough.

With barely controlled anger, he summoned Cardinal Ottaviani and a half-dozen of his conspiratorial Curial brethren to dinner at the Apostolic Palace. After a spartan meal in which little of consequence was discussed, Pope John rose and beckoned his guests to accompany him for a walk. They made their way to the Vatican Museum and entered the extensive Gallery of Maps. As they proceeded through the vast collection of floor-to-ceiling frescoes depicting geographical renderings from various millennia, John suddenly stopped and surveyed the cavernous hallway surrounding them.

"I can only wonder," Pope John said to his small gathering, raising his arm in a wide, circular arc, "how mysterious God's creation must have seemed to these ancient mapmakers. Such a wondrous world lay beyond their borders that they simply could not comprehend." He paused as they all scanned the magnificent collection. "Yet they had faith, they dared to imagine." He let this thought sink in for a moment as the cardinals regarded the fantastic depictions of the world as it had been perceived in ancient times.

The group then continued walking slowly and silently amidst the beautifully detailed paintings and charts with their magical inlays of elaborate compasses, dreadful sea creatures, and flailing ships battling tempests. The barrel-vaulted ceiling, so magnificent in its own architectural right and decorated with stucco, gold leaf, grotesques, and frescoes, depicted stories from the lives of the saints. The windows to the right afforded breathtaking twilight views of the Vatican gardens and St. Peter's imposing statue centered within.

As they approached the north side of the vast corridor, Pope John led them through a little-known and rarely-used doorway that ascended to the Tower of the Winds, originally commissioned by Pope Gregory XIII in 1578 to secretly determine the extent of inaccuracy in the Julian Calendar, which had been in use since the First Council of Nicaea in 325. Pope John, acting as a tour guide, explained that since the early years of Christianity, Easter had been celebrated on the first Sunday after the first full moon after the spring equinox, March 21st, when day and night were exactly the same. However, during the Council of Trent in 1563 it was discovered that the Julian Calendar was slightly off. The carefully designed room in which they now stood had only a single, tiny window that allowed a ray of sunlight to project onto a marble meridian on the floor. At exactly noon on the spring equinox, according to the Julian Calendar, the ray was supposed to fall on March 21, but instead it fell on March 11; in effect, after 1,200 years, the Julian Calendar had therefore accumulated an error of ten days. At the risk of his own excommunication, Pope Gregory thus proclaimed in 1582 that October 4 that year would be immediately followed by October 15, and the so-called "Gregorian Calendar" has been in use ever since.

"It is amazing," Pope John told his guests, "how the smallest of windows can shed light on the greatest of truths." He once again paused for effect.

"And," he then quipped, looking directly at each of the cardinals in turn, "how rarely a calendar, or other *decision*, is changed once a pope determines its merits."

The Curial officials looked at one another. No one said anything as the group proceeded outside into the Vatican gardens, beautifully lit with subtle tapers along the winding pathways.

"Let me be clear," the pope told the cardinals before bidding them farewell. "The light of truth cannot be ignored. And Vatican Council II *will* commence – not by *your* calendar but by *mine*."

A single light could be seen in an upper floor room of the Accademia Alfonsiana. It was close to midnight and Murphy had finally begun writing, in procrastinated anticipation of his meeting the next day with John Chapin, who had been touring Italy but had returned to Rome prior to his flight back to the States. Murphy intended to present him with a draft of his explosive insights regarding

the subterfuge of the cardinals in the Curia, in particular
Cardinal Ottaviani, as they were attempting to undermine
Pope John's efforts to convene Vatican Council II.

Murphy's article began:

> Four years after assuming control, Pope John still
> leaves even the trained observer perplexed. He is
> a man of simple tastes and habits. Along with the
> portly physique of the northern Italian peasant, he
> exhibits a kindly garrulousness, which seeps through
> his every appearance in St. Peter's or the Vatican.

He paused, smiling at his audacity for calling out the
pope's rotundity. But it was true.

> Yet despite his advanced age (in November he will
> have completed his eighty-first year), despite the
> precariousness of world conditions, despite the
> hesitations of his predecessor, a man admittedly far
> more astute than he, despite the internal opposi-
> tion (but outward acquiescence) of his Secretary of
> State, who, they say, died of chagrin at his inability
> to soften or deflect the original decision, Pope John
> will open the Twenty-first Ecumenical Council in St.
> Peter's Basilica on October 11, 1962.

Murphy muttered to himself with satisfaction as he
re-read his introductory lines. He continued:

Pope John's original plan looked to the Fall of 1963 for the convocation, and it is said here that he actually advanced the target date for the Council each time a Vatican official approached him with a suggestion for postponing it. After their first incredulous reactions, his immediate advisers – the members of the Curia, which is roughly the equivalent of a political Cabinet – were appalled at his dismissal of their objections concerning the amount of time and the complex preparations needed for such a step. If the advocates of postponement were prompted by the hope that eternity would beat Pope John to the punch (he was chosen as a "compromise candidate" with an anticipated short reign), they apparently have only themselves to blame for the fact that the Council is opening one year earlier than planned.

Murphy examined these lines, smiled, then continued writing. After providing some historical background on previous Vatican Councils, which he thought necessary for an American readership, he plunged right into what he considered the heart of the matter – the intransigence and subterfuge of the ultra-conservative cardinals within the Curia who were hell-bent on stopping any efforts by Pope John to bring the Catholic Church up-to-date in the modern world.

Many believe that the time has come to break the stranglehold on ecclesiastical thought and operations exercised by the self-perpetuating clique of Roman Curial officials, who, as heads and administrators of the various Congregations that make up the Curia, dictate Roman Catholic policy and, to a large extent, control the pope himself. These men have successfully resisted all but the most innocuous changes dictated by the exigencies of modern life. To these men, the announcement of the Council came as a severe shock....

Time was flying now, as was Murphy's pen.

Although the new Council was the last thing in the world that the old guard Vatican officials in the Curia desired, once they were convinced of the pope's determination to go ahead they proved themselves not without resources. Enjoying the advantage of being on the spot and in control of Vatican activities, they quickly rallied to dominate the Preparatory Commissions that were to organize the Council. They made their trusted friends the presidents and the secretaries, inviting at first only "safe" men from other parts of the world to sit in as experts....

A close look at the *Annuario Pontificio,* which is the official yearbook of the Vatican, reveals a curious fact that is at the heart of the present difficulties within the Church. The twelve Roman Congregations of the Curia, though each is headed by a cardinal, are controlled by an interlocking directorate of bishops and monsignors, all Italian. The assessor, or administrative director, of the Congregation of the Holy Office, for example, is the controversial Archbishop Pietro Parente, who was actually expelled from Rome by Pope Pius XI. His job might be compared to that of J. Edgar Hoover. His is one of a host of Italian names that appear on every other page of the part of the *Annuario* that is devoted to the Roman Curia....

Over the last few years, the Roman Curialists would seem to have been devising a plan to give themselves absolute control over the Church's intellectual life....

When the conclave elected the seventy-six-year-old diplomat and Patriarch of Venice, who became Pope John XXIII, the men of the Roman Curia must have breathed a sigh of relief. They were no doubt convinced that Divine Providence was on their side. The new pontiff was not an intellectual. He made no pretense of being a theologian. With a little careful maneuvering, they could have their way....

The history of the great Councils of the Church is far from edifying. Not one of the twenty previous Ecumenical Councils was achieved without a clash of ideas – and occasionally of fisticuffs....[1]

Murphy continued writing until well past sunrise; he was spent, he needed to lie down and rest. An article like

---

[1] "Letter from Vatican City," *The New Yorker*, October 20, 1962

this, exposing the political infighting within the Vatican walls, had never been published in the lay American press, and certainly not in a venue as prestigious as his intended publication, *The New Yorker*. However, in this instance, Murphy thought passionately, the future of the Catholic Church was at stake.

"This is unbelievable," John Chapin said to Father Murphy at a crowded café on a side street just off the Via della Conciliazione. Murphy was uncomfortable with its proximity to the Vatican, but it was Chapin's choice given the nearness to his hotel.

"Where did you get all this?" Chapin queried uneasily.

"I can't answer that," responded Murphy coyly, with a smile. "Let's just say a combination of observation and contacts in the right places."

Chapin inhaled. "Well, what do you intend to do with this?" he asked, tapping his finger on Murphy's draft article.

"I want the truth to get out there. The cardinals in the Curia are living in the past, the ancient past, and they are determined to suffocate even the smallest efforts by Pope John to address the critical issues facing the Catholic Church today. I can't just sit back and watch them succeed."

"You want this published?"

"Yes."

"Where did you have in mind?"

"*The New Yorker.*"

Chapin let out a soft whistle. "*The New Yorker? The New Yorker!* What about some religious magazine … or even *The Saturday Evening Post?*"

"No. This is too important. It needs to be *The New Yorker.*"

"But what about *you*? How can you do this? What will happen to you when it's published?"

"I've thought about that. I took an Oath of Secrecy at the start of the preparations for the Council. We all did, from cardinals on down. So nobody can know it's me. I can't possibly use my real name. They would shut me down immediately."

"Or worse?" queried Chapin with honest concern, neither one of them broaching the realistic threat of excommunication.

"Yes."

"And you still want to proceed?" Chapin asked again, trying to give Murphy an opportunity to back out.

"Absolutely!" Murphy responded emphatically to reassure Chapin of his resolve. "Ottaviani and his gang are *never* going to let up," he said with anger, "so I'll have plenty more where this came from."

Chapin picked up the article then stood up to leave. "I'll be flying home tomorrow. I know an editor in New York, a guy named Bob Giroux. I'll give him a call and see what he thinks." He then added, "But the repercussions … for you personally," Chapin reiterated again, "they'll come after you." He sat back down in his chair and lowered his voice. "So you want to use a pseudonym?"

Murphy thought for a moment. "What about Xavier Rynne? My mother's maiden name is Rynne and my middle name is Xavier," he offered with very little forethought.

"If that's what you want, we can give it a try. I'll be in touch."

———◆———

The cardinals of the Curia looked upon the upcoming Council with horror. As they saw it, Pope John simply did not understand the potentially catastrophic implications of overturning centuries-held Church doctrines to address fleeting contemporary issues. Furthermore, there were growing calls from many outside of Vatican City, all of whom would be in attendance at the upcoming Council, to finally subjugate the Curia and reform its antiquated doctrinal policies and procedures. Pope Pius XII, toward the end of his papacy, had made his own concerted effort to reign in the powers and influence of the Curia, but to no avail. His rapidly failing health – combined with well-orchestrated Curial delaying tactics in anticipation of his passing – had precluded any meaningful progress toward that end.

In the weeks leading up to the official opening of Vatican Council II, thousands of prelates began descending upon Rome from extraordinarily varied geographic and cultural backgrounds. They ranged from vicars of the smallest of flocks, such as Bishop Gunnarsson of Holar, Iceland, with only 806 Catholics, to that of Albert Cardinal Meyer of Chicago, with 2.1 million. They approached the practice of the faith in remarkably creative ways, from Bishop Willem Van Bekkum of Ruteng in Indonesia, who adapted ceremonies of Confirmation to local tribal customs, to Bishop Cornelius Chitsulo of Dedza, Nyaaland, who translated the Roman Rite of the Mass into the Cinyanja language. Emanuel Mabathoana, the Bishop of Maseru, was the grandson of the "Lion of the Mountain," a tribal chief of the Basutos in South Africa. Bishop Pius Bonaventure Dlamini of Umzimkulu was a member of the royal family of Natal. Valerian Cardinal Gracias of Pakistan lived among the poor in the slums of Karachi. Archbishop Boleslaw Kominek of Poland was the son of a Silesian miner. Bishop Ruben Salazar of Colombia turned his palace in Medellín, a gift from his family, into a school for laborers, living himself in a shed in one of the barrios on the edge of town.

As Pope John watched them all arrive and get settled prior to the start of the Council, he marveled at their diversity and looked forward to the many wonderful new viewpoints that would soon be shared among them. While the curmudgeons in the Curia, as Pope John had begun calling them, railed that Vatican Council II would show the world at large how disunited the Catholic Church had become, he had a completely different perspective – one of *aggiornamento*, of bringing the Catholic Church up-to-date in a rapidly modernizing world. When asked in one audience by a newly arrived cardinal to define the overall purpose of the Council, Pope John simply smiled, went to the nearest window, opened it wide, and let in the fresh air.

———◆———

"Father Murphy speaking," he answered as he took the call in his room at the Accademia Alfonsiana.

"Hello Father, my name is Bob Giroux, an editor with Farrar, Straus, and Cudahy in New York.[2] John Chapin gave me a copy of your article on the preparations for Vatican Council II. Do you have a minute?"

"Of course, Mr. Giroux." It was 11:30 p.m. in Rome, 5:30 p.m. in New York. Murphy had just returned to his residence from an extended dinner and late night of drinks with friends.

"Please call me Bob," Giroux said, audibly clearing his throat. "If I may be honest, Father, this is pretty explosive stuff. Paints some people in a pretty bad light. Can I ask where you got your information? And is it accurate?"

"Completely accurate, Bob. And I'm well connected over here. I know lots of people in the right places."

"So you're *absolutely* confident in its veracity?"

"Yes. *Absolutely.*"

After a long, thoughtful pause, Giroux continued. "Well, that's what John Chapin told me. And I trust his judgment," he responded, albeit still a bit uncertainly. "I also understand there is some type of vow of secrecy involving all proceedings related to the Council, is that correct?"

---

[2] Soon to become Farrar, Straus, and Giroux in 1964 when Robert Giroux is named a partner.

"Yes," responded Murphy, now getting uncomfortable. "And your position on that?"

Murphy sighed audibly into the phone. "Bob, let me be honest," he said, his Irish ire rising. "There are forces at work here, very strong ones, that are determined to keep the Catholic Church in the Dark Ages, to prevent any progress at all. If they have their way, they will sabotage this Council from the get-go. I can't let that happen. I won't let that happen. I want people to know the truth."

"At the risk of breaking your vow to the Council? At your own personal risk?" pursued Giroux.

"Absolutely," Murphy responded firmly.

After a long pause, Giroux sighed. "Okay then," he said. "I've actually already passed your article on to Bill Shawn, an editor at *The New Yorker,* and he has accepted it on my recommendation. But I just had to make sure... to confirm what Chapin told me. I'll give Shawn the green light to contact you for more details. Is that okay?"

"It most certainly is."

"Well then, thank you, Father. We'll keep in touch."

"No, thank *you,*" Murphy said as he hung up the phone, somewhat in disbelief and nowhere near as cocksure as he had been only a few minutes earlier now that the risk of his surreptitious undertaking was becoming a reality. He looked out of his single dormitory window at the overcast night sky, not a star visible because of thickening cloud cover. He opened the window, breathing deeply and taking in the cool night air. "Here we go," he muttered to himself, a bit uncertainly. "Here... we... go."

The next day La Carbonara was crowded, somewhat unusual for the early evening, and Murphy had to wait for a couple to pay their bill before a seat at the bar opened up. He slid in and ordered a scotch, his first of many that night, to calm himself. Cristina, who was serving a table at the far end of the restaurant, noticed his arrival and winked flirtatiously. Murphy saw but barely acknowledged her. When she had taken the table's order, she hurried up to the bar and playfully embraced Murphy from behind. He didn't respond, to her disappointment. She let him be, went to place the order, and then continued on to other tables. She returned about ten minutes later and Murphy was already finishing his second scotch, noticeably calmer.

"What is it, *caro amico*?" she offered affectionately.

At this he did respond, taking her hand and apologizing. "I'm fine, my dear, just fine," he said, smiling weakly. Catching himself, however, he quickly changed his demeanor. "I am really sorry, just a very busy day," he said with half-hearted enthusiasm. "It looks like you're busy too," he added, pointing to the completely full restaurant.

She took the hint. "Yes…very busy. I'll be back later," she said and off she went.

Murphy felt bad. It wasn't like him, especially with Cristina, with whom an intriguing relationship seemed to be unfolding. But a creeping fear was overtaking him, the weight of his actions as Xavier Rynne suddenly becoming very real. Was he doing the right thing? Was there a better way? After a third scotch he had calmed down considerably, gathering conviction in the process. He paid his tab, called Cristina over, gave her an effusive hug and apologized again. Then he walked slowly back to his apartment at the Accademia Alfonsiana.

He ascended the narrow stairs to the fourth floor. All was quiet in the hallway as he put the key into his door, always locked in his absence, a surprising habit to his fellow Redemptorists but one they dismissed as a quirky Americanism. He entered and went quickly to the telephone at his desk. After an interminable effort getting through the Italian switchboard operator, he was finally connected to Bill Shawn, who would be his editor at *The New Yorker*.

He inhaled to compose himself. "Bill, it's Father Murphy," he said, still partially out of breath.

There was a pause at the other end.

"It's Father Murphy." Still no response. "Rome? Xavier Rynne?"

"Oh. Of course, of course!" replied Shawn. "Sorry about the hesitation. I wasn't expecting your call; you caught me by surprise. But, quite frankly, I'm glad you did. Your article will create quite the firestorm – not only in New York but throughout the States."

"Likely in Rome as well," Murphy responded with poorly-concealed trepidation.

Sensing this, Shawn queried, "Are you okay? Any regrets? Do you want out?" There was a crackle in the connection but it held.

"No," replied Murphy. "I still want you to run with it, in full."

Shawn persisted, "Father, I have to ask again. Are you really sure about this? It's great stuff, inside Vatican stuff, never before touched by us or any other mainstream publication stateside. But there's no risk for us. It's all on *you*. Are you *sure*?"

"Absolutely," replied Murphy, with a bit more conviction. "There is a lot at stake."

"Okay then," said Shawn. "It's scheduled for print to coincide with the opening of the Council." Shawn could hear a faint exhale from the other receiver. "But one more thing… and I'm not sure how to approach this with a priest. There will be some significant royalty payments coming your way. How do you want to handle them?"

"The checks can come to me personally," answered Murphy. "There is no problem. I have it covered. Thank you."

"No, thank *you*," replied Shawn. "I hope the risk is worth it."

CHAPTER V

—◆—

"Prophets of Doom"

Anyone with the good fortune to be standing in the piazza fronting St. Peter's Basilica in Rome at eight a.m. on October 11, 1962, was treated to a pageant of dazzling splendor. Suddenly the bronze doors of the Apostolic Palace were thrown open by two papal gendarmes, resplendent in traditional parade regalia of white trousers, black knee-high topboots, formal coats, and fur-lined, plumed busbies atop their heads. Out poured a torrent of light. Then, descending from the majestic Scala Regia staircase, row upon row of bishops clad in flowing white damask copes and mitres marched across the sun-bathed square, wheeled right, and disappeared into the vast basilica.

Every now and then, this sea of white was dotted with a black cassock, full beard, and cylindrical headdress of an oriental patriarch, and here and there with the bulbous gold crown and crossed pectoral reliquaries of bishops of the Byzantine Rite. Toward the end came the scarlet ranks of the Sacred College of Cardinals of the Roman Catholic Church.

Climaxing this splendor was Pope John XXIII, seated on the ancient ceremonial *sedia gestatoria* being carried aloft by twelve footmen. He looked uncomfortable, almost scared, until he suddenly reacted to the hurrahs of the immense crowd which trailed down the Via della Concil-iazione. As he was conveyed up the steps leading into St. Peter's, tears trickled down his face. He had lived to fulfill his dream. Vatican Council II had begun.

———◆———

Seated at the base of the high altar in the majestic basilica, framed and appearing small underneath Berni-ni's imposing Baldacchino canopy, John XXIII looked out upon the overflowing congregation of more than 2,500 church leaders from around the world, their mitred heads visible in tier upon tier of lateral rows filling the vast nave. To his immediate right at the altar sat his nemesis, Alfredo Cardinal Ottaviani, who was uncertain as to why he had been given this remarkable honor. Nonetheless, Ottavi-ani sat staunchly erect, as if this placement was his public due. To the pope's left and to the sides of the altar were the other members of the Vatican Curia, similarly imperious in posture.

The pope's golden, ornately embroidered mitre, the tall hat given to every bishop of the Church, fell too low on his head, with his ears poking out almost comically as if to prevent it from farther descent. In contrast, Cardinal Otta-viani's gleaming white mitre was perfectly aligned in place. When Pope John was handed the copy of his speech, he delicately put on his reading glasses and, although remaining seated, slouched forward toward a newly-placed microphone. He was uncomfortably constricted in layer upon layer of his formal papal vestments. Next to him, Cardinal Ottaviani was confidently scanning the crowd, taking in the spectacle. The lighting throughout the basilica was muted, except directly over the altar, illuminating the contrasting pair of clerics. The air was close, almost claustrophobic, palpably heavy with anticipation.

In initially hesitant but then surprisingly resonant tones for the clearly ailing eighty-year-old pontiff, John could be distinctly heard by all. After a few introductory remarks, he suddenly paused, slowly scanned the group of Curial cardinals upon the altar, then looked up at the extraordinary expanse of global Church hierarchy before him. He continued in distinct, carefully measured words: "I am tired of listening to all of the naysayers among my advisors," he said firmly, catching the entire assemblage by surprise. The cardinals seated adjacent to him, most notably Cardinal Ottaviani, suddenly shifted uneasily in their seats, paying close attention. "Though burning with zeal," Pope John said, "these men are not endowed with very much sense of discretion or measure." He paused again, allowing the import – shock – of his comments to sink in. "They maintain that our era, in comparison with past eras, is getting worse, and they behave as though they have learned nothing from history, which is the great teacher of life." John paused again and an unmistakable murmur began rolling throughout the gathered congregation. "We feel that we must disagree with these *Prophets of Doom*," he said with emphasis, "who are always forecasting disaster, as though the end of the world were at hand, that the modern world is full of prevarication and ruin."

All eyes were unconsciously drawn toward Cardinal Ottaviani, who sat completely stone-faced, smoldering.

Then the pope transitioned to why he had called forth the Council, to the visible relief of the still-stunned cardinals on the altar. "Divine Providence," he said, "is leading us to a new order of human relations. It is imperative for the Church to bring herself up-to-date, to view with an open and honest lens new conditions and ways of life that have been introduced into the modern world." He paused again, looking up for effect, then continued reading. "In so doing, the Church must make use of the medicine of mercy rather than that of severity, to meet the needs of the present day by demonstrating the validity of her teaching rather than by condemnation." This was an unmistakable disavowal of the inquisitorial approach of the Holy Office led by Cardinal Ottaviani, who was now visibly fuming, yet he could do nothing.

Pope John then closed his address by calling for a movement toward unity among all religions, Christian and non-Christian alike, and for putting deep-rooted, centuries-old animosities aside. This was an extraordinarily bold overture that was met with spontaneous applause by everyone within the basilica – with the notable exception of those members of the Curia seated on the altar nearest to him, whose feigned polite claps spoke volumes.

———— ◆ ————

Father Francis X. Murphy had secured a prime ticket for the Opening Ceremony of Vatican Council II and found himself in the crowded upper balcony overlooking the vast array of clerics in the tiered rows below. A few days earlier he had heard that the aging and infirm Bishop Aloysius Willinger of Fresno, California, was in need of an assistant to attend Council meetings on his behalf and report back to him. Murphy saw a golden opportunity to gain *carte blanche* access to all of the proceedings of the Council as Willinger's *peritus* or personal expert, and he seized upon it.

Murphy sat awestruck at the spectacle before him: the white cassocks of the Roman Catholic clerics contrasting so grandly with the regalia of the bishops from the Oriental and Eastern Rite churches; the iconic artwork and rich architectural adornments of St. Peter's Basilica itself; the somber countenances of the powerful cardinals of the Curia immediately surrounding the visibly aged Pope John, who was seated so humbly at the opulently imposing altar. A gathering of such scope and magnitude had never before been attempted in the nearly 2,000-year history of the Roman Catholic Church – and it would certainly not be repeated again in his lifetime.

Murphy had not anticipated such an audacious address by Pope John; no one had, especially given all of the Vatican political in-fighting leading up to the Council that Murphy, under the pseudonym Xavier Rynne, had just detailed so blisteringly in his first article for *The New Yorker*. Those present had all expected a unifying call by Pope John for open-mindedness during the Council proceedings, although in truth very few anticipated actual resolve by the attendees – or even by Pope John himself – to upend the centuries-entrenched status quo.

As Pope John concluded his remarks and slowly made his way down the long central aisle of the basilica, this time ponderously, painstakingly on foot, Murphy watched, transfixed. *Could he do it?* Murphy thought to himself. *Could John really pull this off?*

The very next day Pope John held a small, intimate gathering with visiting journalists in the Sistine Chapel. Speaking in front of Michelangelo's great mural *The Last Judgment*, the pope asked those in attendance to be especially prudent in reporting only the truth about the upcoming proceedings, rather than delving into speculation, rumors, and innuendo. The symbolism of meeting with the journalists under that particular painting could not have been more obvious. John then bade them farewell and moved on to the Hall of Consistory in the Apostolic Palace, where he welcomed the delegates from all of the non-Roman Catholic religions who were attending the Council as observers. Once again, the symbolism was intentional. They were meeting in the ornate, sacred room where Catholic bishops were traditionally elevated to the College of Cardinals, a truly rare privilege. Furthermore, Pope John sat himself in a chair alongside the guests, rather than on the raised papal throne in front. He assured them of his heartfelt welcome and reiterated his ambitious goal for Vatican Council II, *aggiornamento*, which meant bringing the Catholic Church up-to-date in this tumultuous modern world they all shared. He then expressed his hope that their presence would hasten the day when Christ's prayer, "That they may be one," might finally be realized.

One Eastern Orthodox bishop cautiously raised his hand and asked timidly, "Do you truly believe this can be accomplished?"

Pope John was taken aback by that simple yet profoundly important question, one likely on the minds of many now gathered in the hall. He reflected a moment then spoke with absolute conviction, "Yes." He scanned the gathering and continued, "The man who, having chosen a good, or even a great and noble objective, never loses sight of it, but manages to overcome all obstacles and see it through to the end." He closed his eyes, as if in prayer, then added, "He looks to God alone, in whom he trusts, and this is the foundation of all he does."

Upon returning to his papal apartment, John immediately collapsed onto his bed, fully clothed, in pent-up fatigue and well-hidden pain. He lay quietly, grimacing occasionally, his overt confidence dissipating rapidly. A knock on his door startled him; it was Father Capovilla who had followed him to his apartment, conscious of his need to rest but worried nonetheless. By the time that John bade him to enter, the pontiff was sitting upright on the edge of his bed, frail but calm.

"Holy Father, do you need assistance?" Capovilla asked with concern.

"Yes…yes, I do indeed," John answered weakly as he extended his arm to be helped up to a chair, slowly, fitfully.

The next morning, John would watch the proceedings of the Council from his papal apartment on a specially installed closed-circuit television. He would not enter the Council Hall again until the midpoint of the First Session. The reason would soon become apparent to all.

The First Session of Vatican Council II – there would eventually be four in total – took place from October 11 to December 8, 1962. The next three sessions would extend over similar time periods during the subsequent three years, with a 9-month interlude between each session.

The first issue scheduled for debate by the Council was the mandatory use of Latin in all church services around the world, rather than incorporating the local language of each congregation. This was a topic especially dear to Pope John since he had witnessed first-hand the implications when disengaged parishioners were often clueless to the proceedings of the Latin Mass in front of them.

Cardinal Ottaviani, whose Preparatory Theological Commission oversaw the schema outlining how this topic of discussion would proceed, opened the debate by walking confidently up to the microphone and arguing vigorously that Latin was *the* bond of unity shared throughout the worldwide Catholic Church. Ironically, however, Latin was also the official language of the Vatican Council II deliberations and it was becoming readily apparent that not even all of the cardinals in the Curia were sufficiently versed in the tongue, let alone most of the 2,500 clerics in attendance. In fact, the majority of the real work of Vatican Council II would eventually take place in the vernacular shared languages of the participants themselves, rather than in Latin.

After Cardinal Ottaviani finished, more than a dozen incensed prelates rose to passionately express their frustration with the Latin mandate. "What is the harm in a churchgoer actually *understanding* what is taking place upon the altar?" one bishop from Latin America sarcastically intoned. "They might actually comprehend more than we are here!" Laughter and applause ensued, to Cardinal Ottaviani's clear dismay. Each new speaker seemed to build upon his predecessor's remarks, including surprisingly personal attacks toward Cardinal Ottaviani himself. The delegates had clearly been emboldened by Pope John's opening discourse and, if this was any foreshadowing of the debates to follow, an historically explosive Ecumenical Council was about to unfold.

Finally, Archbishop Pietro Parente, the Assessor of the Holy Office and second-in-command to Cardinal Ottaviani in that congregation, had enough. He sternly walked up to the microphone and voiced his irritation with the criticisms being unfairly levelled on the floor. "Many things have been said here," he declared, "which are neither prudent, just, nor consistent." He took a deep breath, his anger rising. "At the Holy Office we are all *martyrs!*" he shouted, pounding his fist repeatedly on the podium. However, instead of the intended shock value, peals of laughter erupted at the ironic image of these modern-day inquisitors complaining of being persecuted. This infuriated Parente, his voice rising exponentially. "After so much work on your behalf, this is the thanks we get?!" He slammed his fist once more on the podium and then stormed out of the basilica.

Father Murphy, sitting in the balcony during this remarkably acrimonious debate, was beside himself with glee. Here were the most powerful members of the Catholic Church hierarchy, those in complete control of the Vatican Curia, being taken to task by a previously ignored yet suddenly impassioned group of clergy from around the world, many of whom had never set foot in Rome before. They were certainly not intimidated by Cardinal Ottaviani, Archbishop Parente, or their Curial cohorts. Murphy took copious notes.

The first article by "Xavier Rynne," detailing the subterfuge of the cardinals in the Curia throughout the preparations for Vatican Council II, hit the newsstands on October 20, 1962, under the headline "Letter from Vatican City."

"Are you kidding me?" Bishop Willinger said in exasperation to his *peritus*, Father Murphy. "What the hell is *this?*" he fumed, shaking a copy of *The New Yorker* in Murphy's face.

It was mere days after the extraordinary discourse by Pope John to officially open Vatican Council II and the two men were seated on the terrace of the quaint Trianon Borgo Pio, a small hotel just a short walk from the Vatican, where Willinger was staying with about twenty other Council attendees.

Willinger bellowed loudly at Murphy, "You are not doing your job!" He ensured that he was clearly heard by everyone nearby, making an intentional spectacle of his anger.

Not certain where this was leading, since it was the first time that the name "Xavier Rynne" had actually appeared in *The New Yorker*, Murphy responded nervously, "What do you mean I'm not doing my job?"

"One of the bishops staying here gave me his copy of *The New Yorker*. As my *peritus*, why didn't *you* give me a copy?" Willinger growled. Murphy professed ignorance about the article. Willinger continued, "He said it details, with unbelievable accuracy, all of the nastiness that took place between the pope and the Curia during the preparations for the Council." Willinger paused, catching his croaky breath. "Go find me a copy. *Now!*"

Murphy did as he was told and scurried off to find a copy of the magazine. Upon his return, he gave it to Willinger, who immediately began to read the article. "What the *hell?*" Willinger bellowed. "WHAT THE *HELL!*" When he finished, he commented loudly to no one in particular, "Who *is* this guy? Where did he get his information?" Murphy did not respond. "This is gonna hit the fan. *Really* hit the fan in the Vatican," Willinger said, shaking his head.

Unbeknownst to either Willinger or Murphy, it already had.

———◆———

Cardinal Ottaviani was apoplectic. "Xavier Rynne?!" he questioned at the top of his lungs to Archbishop Parente, who was seated across the desk from him in his Vatican office. He flung a copy of *The New Yorker* at Parente and hit him in his chest, with it landing in his lap and then falling to the floor. Parente picked it up and looked indignantly at Ottaviani. It was of course the responsibility of the Holy Office to condemn any heresies against the Catholic Church, and this, given the Oath of Secrecy taken by all attendees at the Council, was a blatantly excommunicable offense. "You must find out who he is!" he screamed at Parente. "NOW!" Parente stood, nodded, and took his rapid leave with the magazine firmly clenched in his hand.

It was extraordinary that a man of Pietro Parente's controversial background and mercurial temperament could have been appointed to such a highly sensitive position as that of Assessor, or Chief Inquisitor, of the Holy Office. However, in many ways he was a shadow image of Cardinal Ottaviani himself and thus uniquely qualified for the role.

In the 1930s, as the Rector of the Propaganda College in Rome, Parente had managed to incur the wrath of Pope Pius XI because of his savage, highly personal attacks against anyone who opposed his ultra-orthodox views. Consequently, he was exiled from the Eternal City until Pius XII assumed the papacy. Powerful conservative voices within the Curia lobbied for Parente's return to the Curia, and he was eventually brought back and actually promoted to become the archbishop of Perugia, just north of Rome. Yet, once there, he angered both resident clergy as well as lay parishioners throughout the diocese by aggressively assailing liberal political and social causes well beyond his pastoral mandate. As a result, in 1959 he was "translated" out of that position, but not without benefit. Cardinal Ottaviani had just assumed the leadership of the Congregation of the Holy Office and, recognizing the need for a loyal and unabashedly aggressive assistant to take action against perceived heretical behaviors, he brought Parente in as his Assessor. Within a year of his appointment, Parente had earned the nickname "Hammerer of Heretics."

It would be an apt designation for his fanatical pursuit to unmask the identity of Xavier Rynne.

───────●▬●───────

The rancorous debate on the mandatory use of Latin in all Catholic church services set a dangerous precedent for the Council. After close to a week spent on this issue alone, it became readily apparent that it would be near impossible for the Council to adequately debate the dozen or so schema originally scheduled for the First Session. A further complicating factor was the restrictive parliamentary procedures established during the Preparatory Phase that heavily favored the conservative minority. For example, if the delegates were dissatisfied with any proposed schema, usually because of a blatantly-skewed conservative bias, a two-thirds vote of the entire assemblage was required to reject it. The schema would then have to be returned to its respective Preparatory Commission for further review – a process that could take weeks or months at the sole discretion of that commission's president. Not coincidentally, that task more often than not fell to Cardinal Ottaviani and his Preparatory Theological Commission. Given that there were only eight weeks slated for the entire First Session, this virtually guaranteed that no meaningful progress would be made by its conclusion.

During the critical first weeks of the Council, Pope John had kept himself secluded in his papal apartment, but he did take the time to issue a new proclamation detailing the procedures to be followed upon the death of a pope, apparently to avoid the kind of commercial exploitation that had surrounded Pius XII's recent death and burial. This did nothing to mollify the increasingly widespread rumors about his health. Just the opposite.

Yet John was closely following all of the proceedings of the Council, both on the closed-circuit television that he had installed as well as through regular reporting by Father Capovilla, who was becoming deeply concerned about the dramatic changes in the pope's physical appearance and demeanor.

Growing frustrated with his secretary's constant entreaties about his health, Pope John finally responded, "My father, while tending the farm, would often say, 'Give careful attention to your herd, but keep your distance when the wind shifts.'" John chuckled at this, as did Capovilla uncertainly, until he suddenly took the hint to steer clear of that line of questioning in the future. To Capovilla's subsequent regret, he would not bring up the subject of the pope's health again until it was too late.

When it became all too apparent that the Council had become embroiled in a grinding stalemate, Pope John finally decided enough was enough. He made a rare personal appearance in the Council, delivering a Papal Decree to require henceforth that only a simple majority would be necessary to vote on changes to any schema governing the debates. By unilaterally lowering that critical threshold, he infuriated Cardinal Ottaviani and his Curial brethren. But it immediately broke stalemates for some of the early – and often most contentious – debates. These involved issues like offering wine in addition to bread at communion; allowing concelebration of the Mass by multiple priests on special occasions; extending forgiveness to priests who had broken their vows and left the religious life; exploring the use of modern media to spread the Church's message; and beginning the process of reconciliation with other Christian denominations.

As these debates, now unchained, commenced with renewed vigor, it became increasingly apparent that a majority of the delegates in attendance were clearly leaning in progressive directions. This did not go unnoticed by Cardinal Ottaviani, who saw this as a perilous challenge to the immutable role that he felt was central to Roman Catholic doctrine. At one point, during the debate on including wine in communion at church services, he rose out of turn, stomped up to the podium, and forcefully grabbed the microphone out of the hands of the current speaker.

"Are you Council Fathers planning a revolution?" Ottaviani yelled in response to the "heretically radical" ideas that he was hearing. He warned against confusing, let alone scandalizing, the faithful by introducing so many changes. With rising fury, he maintained that the current motion to have communion under both bread and wine had already been dismissed during the Preparatory Commission stage (by his own Theological Commission), to which a chorus of sarcastic boos could be heard. He then railed against concelebration of a Mass by multiple priests because it made the service "seem like something happening in a theater" (a clear slap at the Eastern Rite churches where concelebration was normal). He also fumed that a priest's final vows should be regarded as sacred; renouncing them should be met with "excommunication, not mercy!" Groans could be heard throughout the basilica.

"Be cautious when contemplating changes to long-established Church practices!" Ottaviani yelled in rising vitriol. "Had not God warned Moses to remove his sandals when approaching the burning bush?"

Catcalls could be heard at that surprising metaphor, but Ottaviani was unfazed. He was about to continue when an Austrian bishop suddenly stood up and shouted from a back row, "If the Church can be modernized merely by removing one's shoes, I would like to be the first to do so!"

Laughter erupted throughout the basilica, met by a scowl of disgust from Cardinal Ottaviani. Then Bernard Cardinal Alfrink of The Netherlands, that day's moderator of the proceedings, politely interposed, "Excuse me, Eminence, but you have already spoken more than the allowed fifteen minutes and…"

Ottaviani rudely cut him off and continued to drone on, getting increasingly agitated as he did so. After an unsuccessful second warning, Alfrink simply unplugged the microphone and those in attendance applauded the bold action. Cardinal Ottaviani was now not only angry but embarrassed, and he stormed out of the basilica.

It was obvious that a seemingly intractable air of dis-harmony had descended upon the Council's proceedings; debates were frequently called off prematurely to calm tempers, after which many of the delegates retired to Bar Jonah, an expansive coffee shop that had been temporarily set up by Pope John within the confines of the Vatican. "If I don't give them a place to smoke, they'll be hiding ciga-rettes under their mitres!" he quipped. There, the multi-tude of cardinals and bishops spoke freely and candidly about each day's debates, sharing personal opinions, col-luding to take concerted actions, and offering unfiltered comments on the fractious behaviors of certain prelates.

Father Murphy was right there among them, taking it all in, picking up news and gossip from the emotion-ally charged churchmen. Then, at the end of each lengthy day, he would head to the bar in La Carbonara to unwind before finally retiring to his apartment in the Accademia Alfonsiana to write it all down, often working well into the night. He was fervently loyal to the Catholic Church and its mission, and especially to the lofty objectives of Vatican Council II to bring the Church up-to-date in the modern world. Murphy was therefore incensed that such a small but extremely powerful group of ultra-conservatives in the Curia were so well positioned to block many, if not all, of the Council's efforts at reform.

After one especially exhaustive day, he took an end seat at the bar at La Carbonara and was greeted enthusiastically, as usual, by Cristina. However, for the past few weeks she had sensed the growing tenseness within the usually gregarious Murphy, and she was becoming concerned.

"What troubles you, Frank?" she asked in their now more intimate way. She waited for a response but none was forthcoming. "Is it me?" she pursued insecurely.

Murphy, surprised at the intrusiveness of the former question and confused about the latter, said, "Nothing... and no, of course not, Cristina." He gave her a quick, dismissive peck on the cheek. She stepped back, worried, and went off to wait on her tables.

Whatever emotional signals were being misread by Cristina, he thought, were trivial compared to his overriding concerns of the moment. The conservative elements in the Curia were strategically coalescing against the Council – and thus against the rapidly weakening Pope John himself. *Could Ottaviani and his gang succeed?* he pondered, almost aloud.

Cristina returned, still upset. "Is there any way I can be of help to you?" she persisted, interrupting his thoughts. Murphy couldn't quite hear her over the din of the patrons.

"I'm sorry?" he responded.

"Please, what is the matter, Frank?" she asked again, nearly in tears.

"With what?" he grumbled, irritated.

"I... I don't know," she said limply.

Feeling guilty at his undeserved coarseness, Murphy shifted on his stool and looked directly into her eyes. They were indeed beautiful – and sincere. She obviously had feelings for him, and it was increasingly mutual. Therefore, she didn't deserve his callous reproach. However, before he could say anything more, she had turned back toward her tables and left him to his brooding.

While most of the topics scheduled for debate during the First Session of Vatican Council II involved practical, day-to-day aspects of the Catholic faith, there was one crucial issue that related to dogma, or official Church doctrine, that Pope John felt had to be addressed before the Church could truly move forward. It concerned how modern-day Christians should interpret and follow God's Will as it was directly revealed to mankind; i.e., the divine sources of Revelation. The debate on this actually extended back more than 400 years.

Pope Paul III had called the Council of Trent in 1545 in response to the Protestant Reformation, led by Martin Luther and others. Among a number of contentious issues, the protesters against the Catholic Church, or "Protestants," as they were called, declared that the *written word* in the Bible was the *only* source of God's Revelation that should be followed by Christians.

In contrast, the Catholic Church hierarchy of that day argued that the *actions of the Apostles* after Jesus' death were *equally important* as they served as living examples of following God's Will. After all, God had spoken directly to the Apostles through the risen Jesus Christ and the Holy

Spirit. Catholic tradition therefore held that priests, and especially the Church hierarchy, were the inheritors of the Apostles' mission and an equal source of God's Revelation, putting a stamp on their importance in interpreting God's word for the faithful.

The Council of Trent actually went one step further. While it acknowledged *both* the Bible *and* what they called "Tradition" were dual sources of God's Revelation, Trent made the crucial distinction that they were *separate* sources of Revelation, as opposed to complementary sources. Why was this important? If they were to be linked, the Council of Trent argued, in essence the Catholic Church would be giving undue credence to the Protestants' contention of the Bible as the *sole* word of God.

This issue was so divisive that, among other factors, it resulted in the cataclysmic split of the Protestants away from the Roman Catholic Church, including the eventual formation of the Lutheran, Reformed, Presbyterian, Anglican and other Christian denominations still in existence hundreds of years later.

In his opening discourse for Vatican Council II, Pope John had called for a movement toward eventual unity among all Christian religions, putting aside centuries-old animosities. That would inevitably have to include some type of reconciliation regarding the divine sources of Revelation. His invitation to these other denominations to attend the Council as observers was therefore an important symbolic step toward this dream. While the pope knew that no full reconciliation could possibly be realized in the near term, there had to at least be a first step. And he was determined to take it.

Cardinal Ottaviani, on the other hand, would have none of it.

In the months leading up to Vatican Council II, a wide range of feedback on how to consider the divine sources of Revelation had been submitted to Cardinal Ottaviani's Preparatory Theological Commission. However, very little seemed to have been included when Ottaviani rose to the podium and presented this schema for debate to the full Council. Ottaviani called any discussion on altering the Church's stance on Revelation "the ultimate heresy." As such, he ignored any revisionist suggestions from his global peers. "Just as the Council of Trent declared hundreds of years ago," he argued vehemently, "these two sources of God's Revelation can *never* be linked!"

As Ottaviani continued reading the proposed schema to the Council, it became clear that he had completely disregarded Pope John's call for "open debate on all issues affecting the Church in the modern world." As he droned on and on with his personal dissertation on the dangers of tampering with this centuries-tested dogma, he was suddenly interrupted by Bishop Joseph Ritter of St. Louis, who yelled out from the audience, "This schema must be rejected!" Exuberant applause greeted Ritter's outburst and, when it finally died down, Ritter challenged Ottaviani directly: "This schema does not reflect the full range of ideas that were submitted to your Preparatory Theological Commission!"

Flustered at the bold intrusion of the American prelate, Ottaviani countered, "Four hundred years ago the Council of Trent held that there were two *separate*, independent sources of divine Revelation directly from God..."

Ritter cut him off. "This draft is full of unjust suspicions and fears," he said. "It should be thrown out!"

Ernesto Cardinal Ruffini, one of Ottaviani's closest colleagues in the Curia, then stood up in his defense. "This schema has been prepared by men who are both eminent and wise. How then can it be rejected outright?" But this only fueled a growing anger directed toward Cardinal Ottaviani and his Preparatory Commission's prejudicial editing.

Julius Cardinal Doepfner of Munich then rose to speak. "The president of the Preparatory Theological Commission," he said, referring directly to Ottaviani, "has informed us that in the preparation of this schema there was a general accord on the part of the participating theologians and prelates. However, the truth is the *complete opposite*," he said with emphasis. "My impression is that the Preparatory Theological Commission was too much under the influence of one opinion, represented by Cardinal Ottaviani. There was no concern for any other ideas!"

Ottaviani, shocked at these personal attacks on his credibility, responded with anger. "It is *not* true that this schema was made in my name!" he shouted. "In the Preparatory Theological Commission all matters that were the subject of discussion or disagreement were put to a vote. It was normal for the opinion of the minority then to be excluded." This last comment elicited widespread groans and whistles, to which Ottaviani responded, "It is *not* true that only one opinion, one school of thought, was represented!"

A chorus of boos erupted. The anger of the assembled prelates had been unleashed. One bishop who had personally participated in the Preparatory Theological Commission's deliberations stood up and said sheepishly, ashamedly, "His Eminence is not telling the truth. All the world knows it."

An uncomfortable silence suddenly enveloped the basilica, only to be broken by the rapid ascent of Archbishop Parente up to the podium. He argued pointedly about the "official procedures" within the Preparatory Theological Commission, how "all opinions were fairly considered," and that "a clear majority" had emerged in support of the present schema on the divine sources of Revelation. However, while he was talking there was loud disparaging of his remarks. He suddenly stopped mid-sentence, fuming, then stomped down from the podium in disgust.

Bishop André Charue of Belgium then approached the microphone, chastising Cardinal Ottaviani and Archbishop Parente for preparing a completely one-sided schema for discussion. "It is not up to the Council to do the work of your commission," he admonished, "but it *is* up to the Council not to set the stage for another Galileo incident!" he said, referring to the historic blunder of the Vatican in punishing Galileo for presenting the truth about the planets revolving around the sun. This linked Cardinal Ottaviani to a remarkably sensitive period in the history of the Catholic Church, which was blatantly intentional and searingly blunt.

Valerian Cardinal Gracias then further eviscerated the credibility of Cardinal Ottaviani's one-sided schema. "The Preparatory Theological Commission has no monopoly on the Holy Spirit and wisdom!" he thundered from his seat.

The debate on the divine sources of Revelation raged on for days, at times turning into an unconstrained verbal free-for-all, yet Cardinal Ottaviani stubbornly refused to withdraw the schema as originally presented, nor to consider even minor proposed amendments.

Finally, Pope John, who had been following the entire episode on his closed-circuit television, had seen enough. He called in Father Capovilla, who noticed the disheartening frustration on the pontiff's face. "We need to put an end to this," he told Capovilla, handing him a note to be forwarded to the Council. It stated that the debate on the divine sources of Revelation was to be closed immediately. He promised that a completely revised schema would be prepared in the intervening months before next year's Second Session and it would be "even-handed and faithful to the open-mindedness of the Council."

In retrospect, Pope John realized that he had given Cardinal Ottaviani a far-too independent hand throughout the Preparatory Phase of the Council – and Ottaviani had played it brilliantly. He was now fearlessly emboldened.

However, as neither one of them could yet foresee, that would prove to be his undoing.

◆

For an institution that prided itself on the keeping of secrecy for thousands of years, it was uncertain if it could preserve one more: Pope John was dying.

Because of his near total absence from the proceedings of the Council, rumors about the pope's health were rampant. Therefore, it was with extreme anticipation that the 2,500 cardinals, bishops and observer-delegates from other religions filled St. Peter's Basilica on Saturday morning, December 8, 1962, to hear Pope John's closing address for the First Session of Vatican Council II.

At 10:15 a.m., the pope arrived at the massive central bronze door of St. Peter's, on foot instead of atop the ancient *sedia gestatoria* that had marked his entrance so grandly at the opening of the Council. This, in itself, was a welcome sign to the assembled clergy. He slowly, haltingly, made his way down the lengthy nave, surrounded on either side by tiered pews and balconies filled with thousands of his religious colleagues, all cheering emotionally and enthusiastically. Many of those present were moved to tears of relief and admiration at the sight of this revered figure, somewhat pale but still vigorous in his movements, as he ascended to the altar and sat down on the ornate, gilded, papal throne. He looked up at the awe-inspiring scene before him, smiled warmly, then clumsily fished

148

for his glasses. When his speech was handed to him, his hands shook ever so slightly. As he began to read his closing address, his voice gradually strengthened from a near whisper to wonderful vibrancy and strength, in stark contrast to his physical demeanor.

He was heartened, Pope John began, that such an historic gathering as Vatican Council II had been successfully convened. He noted that more than 2,500 of his religious brethren had come to Rome for the Council and close to 1,100 had personally spoken during the various debates. He admitted that the Council had gotten off to a disappointingly slow start and that dissensions had arisen. However, he contended, a truly honest debate of important issues affecting the Church had begun. And then, with a warning that did not escape any of his listeners, he referenced the nine months of work ahead to prepare for the Second Session, to take place the following October, as a task "that would be accomplished without *enmity!*"

He acknowledged that the First Session of Vatican Council II had not produced any major conciliar decrees to present to the Church or to the world, yet he firmly believed there had been sufficient gains to justify calling the Council in the first place and trusted that the groundwork had been laid for a fruitful Second Session. A process had now been set in motion, he argued, to bring the Church up-to-date in the modern world – *aggiornamento* – and that in itself was an answer to his most fervent prayers.

Pope John closed his speech quietly, humbly thanking all those present for their passionate and heartfelt work and expressing his wish to personally welcome them all back to Rome in the new year. There was silence throughout the great hall, due in no small measure to the uncertainty of those gathered regarding the pope's visibly diminished health. Nonetheless, as he descended the altar and fitfully made his way back down the central nave, blessing those he passed, a heartfelt ovation began to swell, becoming thunderous as the pope approached the main doors to the basilica. Appearing ever so small beneath that grand archway, he slowly turned around to the gathering, taking it all in, smiling weakly, then departed.

It would be the last time that they would see their beloved pontiff.

Murphy wrote his second article for *The New Yorker* the day after the closing of the First Session. No less explosive than his first missive, it did not hold back on the political subterfuge of the conservative cardinals in the Curia, led by Cardinal Ottaviani, who had succeeded in blocking any substantive progress from being realized during the eight-week session. Murphy felt a renewed sense of determination to counterbalance these scheming efforts by bringing to public light all of their artifice.

He also felt a special urgency, given the many rumors about Pope John's failing health. Without John's vision and leadership, could Vatican Council II realistically continue? Would the conservative forces aligned with

Cardinal Ottaviani win out? Not because of honest debate but rather as a result of one human being's mortality? It was a sadly tragic question that he pondered as the second *New Yorker* article sent shock waves through the American reading public, and even more so throughout the Curial corridors of Vatican City. It read in part:

> Eight weeks ago, as Pope John entered St. Peter's to inaugurate the twenty-first Ecumenical Council, close bystanders saw tears on his face....
>
> The pope, after a few introductory remarks, said that he was tired of listening to the "Prophets of Doom" among his advisors....
>
> As the congregation heard these words, their attention focused irresistibly on the face of Alfredo Cardinal Ottaviani, who is head of the Congregation of the Holy Office, the branch of the Curia (roughly the papal cabinet) that deals with faith, morals, and heresy, and who was seated at the pope's immediate right....
>
> One of the early debates in the First Session involved the mandatory use of Latin in all religious services rather than conducting them in local languages. The dogged Secretary of the Holy Office (whose post in ancient times bore the title of Inquisitor General) rose to ask whether the Council Fathers were planning a revolution. It would scandalize the faithful to introduce such changes, he asserted....

Cardinal Ottaviani is reported to have drawn up a petition to the pope asking him to condemn all those who uttered heresy in the Council....

Despite his papal optimism, there is still considerable anxiety here. Pope John's health is the primary concern, of course, for the work of the Council has only begun. Without his drive and his paternal charity, things could easily be brought to a standstill....[3]

———

As Pope John lay suffering in the last days of his illness, he demonstrated his characteristic humor in a faint, whispered remark to his personal physician: "Do not look so worried. My bags are packed. I am ready to go." He died on June 3, 1963, at 7:49 p.m. At the time of his death, he was eighty-one.

Following an ancient tradition, his brow was ritually tapped three times with a small silver hammer and his given name, Angelo, called out to confirm, when unanswered, his death. Then the room was illuminated, thus informing those outside of what had transpired. He was buried on June 6th in the Vatican grotto. Two wreaths, placed on both sides of his tomb, had been donated by the prisoners of the Regina Coeli prison in Rome and the Mantova jail in Verona, which he had quietly visited numerous times to offer counsel and forgiveness.

---

[3] "Letter from Vatican City," *The New Yorker,* December 29, 1962

The pontificate of John XXIII was brief – four and a half years, the shortest since that of Pius VIII (1829-30) – but its impact would be historic. Against all odds he had fulfilled his promise of launching Vatican Council II and its mission to "tear the curtains down and open the windows of the Church." It was now up to the next pope to finish that monumental task.

CHAPTER VI

"Who the hell is Xavier Rynne?!"

Father Murphy was becoming much more familiar with the issues facing Villa Nazareth, the orphanage in the Pineta Sacchetti section of Rome where he had first met Cardinal Tardini, Pope John's late Secretary of State. He had since been escorted on a number of occasions by the delightfully persistent Luciana, who waited patiently for the First Session of the Council to end before enticing Murphy back into her endeavors on behalf of these children.

What Murphy had come to fully appreciate through the none-too-subtle entreaties of Luciana was that there was indeed a bleak future for the vast majority of these orphans. Unfortunately, since Tardini's passing, there had also been a dramatic waning of interest in – and thus patronage for – the orphanage. Murphy, the son of renegade Irish immigrants fleeing to America, was innately sensitive to their plight and he had already begun sending inquiries to his various contacts in America regarding potential adoption referrals.

Murphy had intended to explore Europe on holiday after the closing ceremony of the First Session, but his personal time was increasingly being taken up with introductions and social gatherings orchestrated by Luciana. If there was ever a stereotypical Roman socialite, it was certainly her. For every event, she picked him up in a two-tone silver-and-gold limousine, her driver "professional and discreet," as she curiously described him to Murphy. She was always dressed exquisitely for each occasion, in contrast to Murphy's simple priestly black suit and Roman collar. As soon as they arrived at a destination, Luciana immediately took Murphy's arm and rarely relinquished it throughout the evening. Afterward, on the way home, she would inevitably curl up close to him in the back seat, enjoying the quiet intimacy after an evening of what seemed like innocuous small talk. However, Murphy knew much of that conversation was likely shrewd groundwork being laid by Luciana in pursuit of her personal end-goal – rescuing as many children as possible from Villa Nazareth. Nonetheless, he was enjoying the entire adventure immensely and was increasingly on board with the evolving plan to help the children find adoptive parents.

Murphy was still free many other nights during this interregnum period between Council sessions. As a result, he could often be found seated at the bar in La Carbonara. With its regular clientele sparse during the Roman summer, only partially supplanted by handfuls of intrepid foreigners exploring well beyond the traditional tourist sites, Cristina was able to spend much more time with Murphy while working the tables. Their flirtations were also becoming more overt and warmly reciprocated, kept only in check by the conspicuousness of the venue and his clerical garb.

He learned that she was the only daughter and the youngest child in an extremely close, devoutly Catholic family of five, with her father, mother, and two older brothers all employed in semi-regular jobs to make ends meet. They were crowded together into a medium-sized flat in a working class neighborhood to the south of the city, about fifteen miles away from La Carbonara. Beyond that, however, Cristina kept the rest of her personal life private, and Murphy respected that boundary. Actually, he was somewhat relieved by it.

———◆———

Very little had been achieved during the First Session of Vatican Council II: a minor decree addressing the role of the media in communicating Church doctrine; and a Constitution on Sacred Liturgy that emphasized the Mass as the source and summit of the Christian life. Both were of minimal importance compared to the explosive issues that had been originally introduced for debate but successfully thwarted by the Ottaviani-led conservative coalition.

Furthermore, with the prolonged illness and eventual passing of Pope John in June of 1963, the mandated follow-up work by the various Council commissions in advance of the Second Session had ground to a halt. Cardinal Ottaviani and the other commission presidents took full advantage of this lack of oversight, confident that they could finally bring this ill-fated Ecumenical Council to an ignominious end.

Murphy, who as Xavier Rynne, detailed it all for the readership of *The New Yorker:*

> The Curial officials in Rome claim to represent the pope, but in practice they appropriate to themselves the papal function of policymaking. Many bishops hesitate to do anything important without first "checking with Rome" – that is, with the Curia. By procrastination in administrative matters and by a close surveillance of what is said and written, the Curia over the years has reinforced its undisputed authority in the Church....
>
> The chief stumbling blocks during the First Session were the rules under which the Council operated. These rules were demonstrably contrived to assure domination of the proceedings at all stages by the Curia....
>
> Cardinal Ottaviani's Theological Commission has assumed an excessive competence, virtually monopolizing the work of the Council in the Preparatory Phase and throughout the First Session....

Meetings of the Theological Commission were conducted in a manner that eliminated the possibility of any influences being brought to bear by those members and experts who disagreed with its head [Cardinal Ottaviani]. No attention was paid to the numerous suggestions that the bishops of the world had submitted in writing, in defiance of the pope's instructions of December 6th. They were simply ignored....[4]

Cardinal Ottaviani was outraged after reading the latest missive from Xavier Rynne in *The New Yorker*. He became obsessed with unearthing the identity of this sacrilegious author who had clearly violated the secrecy of the Council, not to mention calling into question the credibility of the Vatican Curia as well as personally attacking Cardinal Ottaviani himself. "Who the hell is Xavier Rynne?!" he shouted loudly and often to anyone within earshot.

Having had enough, Cardinal Ottaviani summoned Archbishop Parente into his private study in the Congregation of the Holy Office and they set to work. Parente had brought with him the names of all 2,500 cardinals and bishops who had attended the First Session of the Council, as well as the invited guest observers from other religions. They both began to scan the list but quickly realized the process

[4]"Letter from Vatican City," *The New Yorker,* September 28, 1963

of elimination would take weeks, if not months; they simply didn't have that time. They had to unmask and confront Xavier Rynne before any future articles could be written.

"What if," Parente hesitatingly suggested, "we first focus on the American delegates who might be more familiar with *The New Yorker*?"

Uncharacteristically, Ottaviani smiled at Parente and said, "An excellent idea. Start with Cardinals Meyer of Chicago, Cushing of Boston, Spellman of New York…"

"McIntyre of Los Angeles…and O'Boyle of Washington, DC," Parente added.

"Yes," Ottaviani acknowledged. "They are the most likely to have connections with the American press," he said, before dismissing Parente to follow up.

Three days later, Parente returned to Cardinal Ottaviani, disheartened. "Your Eminence," he began, "I do not think any of them are Xavier Rynne." He could see the angry scowl forming on the cardinal's face yet he had no choice but to continue.

"By far the most staunchly conservative cardinal in America is Cardinal McIntyre of Los Angeles," Parente began. "Prior to the Council he expressed strong reservations about its potential reforms. And during the First Session he rose to argue for the preservation of Latin in religious services, stating, 'The Latin Mass is a treasure of our Church. It is a source of spiritual richness and stability. We must not abandon it hastily.'"

Parente continued, "Spellman of New York and O'Boyle of Washington were both considered somewhat conservative going into the Council but their leanings seem to be changing. For example, during one debate toward the end of the First Session, Spellman spoke in favor of gradual reform: 'We are not making a new Church, we are making a new altar cloth.' O'Boyle also expressed cautious support for reform: 'While we must embrace necessary changes, we must also remember the Church's rich tradition and continuity. Let us move forward with both courage and prudence.'"

Parente concluded, "Neither Spellman nor O'Boyle, and certainly not McIntyre, are passionately progressive enough to be Xavier Rynne."

"And the others?" asked Ottaviani impatiently.

Somewhat perturbed at the unnecessary interruption, Parente proceeded.

"Cushing of Boston and Meyer of Chicago are much more liberal. In the debate on liturgical reform, Cardinal Cushing said, 'We must bring down the walls of Jericho that separate the people from the altar. We must make the Mass a truly communal experience for all the faithful.' Similarly, in the debate on maintaining Latin in the Mass, Cardinal Meyer came down forcefully saying, 'The people have a right to hear the Word of God in their own language. Only then can they truly participate in the liturgy and understand its meaning.'"

He added, "In spite of the above, both men have expressed their support for encouraging a wide range of views to be presented at the Council – both progressive and conservative. While they certainly hope for significant reforms in the Church going forward, they are strong proponents of open debate."

Parente hesitated to conclude, "In my opinion, neither one is polarized enough to present as Xavier Rynne."

Ottaviani pondered what Parente had said.

"Should we begin looking at the *bishops* of the American delegation?" Parente nervously suggested.

Cardinal Ottaviani nodded. "Look at *every single one* of them," he growled. Then he quoted from his favorite passage of Ezekiel in the Old Testament: "I will soon pour out my wrath upon you, and spend my anger against you, and judge you according to your ways, and I will punish you for all your abominations."

Parente bowed and exited with a sinister grin.

The conclave to elect Pope John XXIII's successor commenced on June 19, 1963. Due to the number of new cardinals elevated during John's pontificate, it would be the largest ever assembled in the history of the Roman Catholic Church – eighty. Of these, more than half (forty-five) had been appointed by Pope John. This was worrisome to the conservative elements of the cardinalate because a majority of their newly-elevated brethren were seemingly progressive in their leanings and far too many were non-Italian. Nonetheless, Cardinal Ottaviani, now seventy-two and the Dean of the College of Cardinals, had learned valuable lessons from the papal conclave five years prior. He would not make the same mistakes again.

In spite of his lofty new position as Cardinal Dean, Ottaviani did not go out of his way to welcome – and discretely assess – the incoming delegates, many of whom were new to a conclave. From his viewpoint, after John's debilitating illness and dramatic failure with the First Session, the conclave would almost certainly settle on a younger, stronger papal candidate; in Ottaviani's mind, Cardinal Siri, now five years older, would be the absolute frontrunner. Thus, with unflinching confidence, he relaxed his guard.

As in all conclaves, a single ballot was taken on the first day, with four on each subsequent day (two each in the morning and afternoon), until a candidate received the requisite two-thirds majority for elevation to the papacy. Surprisingly, at least from Cardinal Ottaviani's perspective, Giovanni Cardinal Montini, a favorite of Pope John's because of his strong support for Vatican Council II, was the dominant early vote-getter. Alarmed, Ottaviani and his cohorts began campaigning aggressively against Montini, only to be consistently rebuffed by a reenergized movement of liberal cardinals determined to push back against their political bullying. In fact, even Gustavo Cardinal Testa, himself a conservative member of the Curia, became so incensed by their tactics that he lost his temper and lashed out in an unrestrained rebuke, demanding that they immediately stop attacking Montini's candidacy. In response, Ottaviani and his colleagues only dug in harder, but to no avail, even after Cardinal Montini offered to withdraw his candidacy to keep peace within the conclave.

Throughout the voting on the second day, it became increasingly apparent that in spite of Ottaviani's lobbying efforts Montini would easily attain sufficient votes for elevation to the Throne of St. Peter. Ottaviani resigned himself to that imminent outcome with the knowledge that Montini, throughout his long service as a Vatican bureaucrat, had developed a reputation as a compromiser, someone with little independent conviction, a conflict-avoider at all costs. Thus, in Ottaviani's mind, he could be easily manipulated.

Montini's election became a mere formality on the first morning ballot of the third day of the conclave, the sixth ballot overall. When asked if he accepted his election, Montini replied, "I accept in the name of the Lord, and choose to be known as Pope Paul VI in honor of the Apostle Paul, whose evangelical nature I wish to embody."

The news that the Roman Catholic Church had a new pope broke unexpectedly on Friday, June 21, 1963, at precisely 11:18 a.m. as white smoke ascended through the temporary Sistine Chapel chimney pipe installed for the conclave. Shortly thereafter, when the tall glass doors behind the balcony above the portico of St. Peter's were opened and the red-bordered white papal tapestry, still bearing Pope John's Coat of Arms, was draped over the balustrade, the crowd roared in anticipation. As the procession of cardinal-elders filed onto the balcony and the imposing figure of Cardinal Ottaviani was ushered to the microphone, silence enveloped the thousands of gathered faithful. In a clear and slightly tremulous voice, the cardinal chanted, "I announce to you a great joy. We have a pope! *Giovanni Battista...*Montini!" Only the rising burst of the "Mon-" was heard, but it was sufficient. The crowd exploded. Cardinal Ottaviani impatiently waited for well over a minute, then resumed, "...who has taken the name *Paulum Sextum!"* There was another eruption from the piazza below. Then, along with rest of the scarlet-clad retinue, Cardinal Ottaviani withdrew, leaving the glass doors ajar. The man who had just become Pope Paul VI appeared and advanced hesitantly to the front of the balcony. With just the slightest indication of a smile on his lips, he accepted the acclamation of the crowd.

The new Holy Father began the formulaic blessing to the city of Rome and to the world. "Blessed be the name of the Lord!" rang out in the new pope's strong, melodious voice.

Then, as Pope Paul turned slowly and majestically in a three-quarter circle with sweeping signs of the cross, he sang out, clearly and precisely, "May the blessing of Almighty God, the Father, Son, and Holy Spirit, descend upon you and remain with you forever." This was met with a resounding "Amen!" from the delirious throng.

Father Murphy was not in the grand piazza fronting St. Peter's to witness the presentation of Pope Paul VI. He, along with many others, had not anticipated such a brief conclave.

On this particular day, Murphy and Luciana were tour-ing a vegetable field behind the Villa Nazareth orphanage where dozens of boys and girls and a quartet of nuns in oppressively layered habits were toiling in the summer heat. Yet none were complaining. With any fruits of their labors still months away in what they hoped would be a bountiful fall harvest, Murphy couldn't help but be impressed and empathetic. However, their tasks were sud-denly interrupted by shouts and cheering coming from inside the orphanage. Soon enough, a breathless boy ran toward them with the wonderful news, "We have a pope! We have a new pope!"

<hr />

After Pope Paul's blessing from the balcony, he returned to the Sistine Chapel and formally closed the conclave, after which he invited all of the cardinals to join him for lunch at the extensive table set up for conclave meals in the Borgia apartments. He intentionally sat not at the head of the table but in his old seat, sending an early symbolic message to his brethren. At the end of the meal, instead of waiting the customary few days before moving into the sealed-off private apartment vacated by his predecessor, he insisted on taking residence right away.

That night, Romans noticed lights in the papal apart-ment on the third floor, windows that had been dark for eighteen days. Pope Paul was at his desk writing, in his own hand, a draft of the speech that he would deliver the next day over television to reaffirm that Vatican Council II would indeed continue. He set the date for the opening of the Second Session for Sunday, September 29, 1963, much sooner than had been expected by even the most optimistic observers.

Cardinal Ottaviani was wary. He knew Pope Paul well, having served with him in the Curia for decades. Paul, then-Archbishop Montini, had garnered a mediocre reputation as a Vatican bureaucrat, exasperating his superiors by, ironically, trying too hard to please them and rarely taking a strong, independent stand. He was also more progressive than virtually all of his conservative Curial colleagues. It was only in recent years that he had garnered a true mentor, albeit a very powerful one, in Pope John XXIII. Now, however, Pope Paul was on his own, at an historic crossroads in the history of the Catholic Church, and Ottaviani was determined to exploit his every vulnerability.

The new pope was sixty-five. He was not physically imposing, standing only 5' 8" and bordering on slight, with a hawkish nose and deep-set eyes. He was studious in nature with a keen intellect, and was gracious and genteel in his bearing. He was quiet, reserved, and surprisingly timid for the extraordinary office he now held.

Giovanni Battista Enrico Antonio Maria Montini was born in Concesio, a suburb of Brescia, in northern Italy, to a family belonging to the professional class. His father had edited the local daily newspaper, *Il Cittadino*, for twenty-five years and had served three terms in the Italian Parliament before the era of Fascism. The young Montini had first undertaken his studies for the priesthood privately (as had Pius XII) and then in the nearby seminary. He was ordained a priest on May 29, 1920, and immediately entered into the papal foreign service school for diplomatic training. In 1923, he was sent to Warsaw as a minor official in the Holy See's nunciature, its equivalent of a diplomatic mission. However, while on station he suddenly became severely ill with an undiagnosed ailment and was brought back to Rome to recuperate. He was then given duties in the Vatican Secretariat of State, one of the most important departments in the Curia, where he worked unremarkably in various capacities for the next three decades. He was the ultimate Curial bureaucrat, having never once served as a parish priest.

By the outbreak of World War II, however, Monsignor Montini had risen to become a relatively powerful administrator within the Vatican Secretariat, due in no small measure to his simple longevity within it, and it was assumed that either he or Monsignor Domenico Tardini would succeed the aging and infirm Luigi Cardinal Maglione as the Vatican Secretary of State. However, given the turbulent times, Pope Pius XII decided to function as his own Secretary of State and named his two chief aides, Montini and Tardini, as his under-secretaries.

Tardini aligned himself with the more conservative members of the Vatican Curia, including then-Monsignor

Ottaviani of the Holy Office. Montini, on the other hand, took a more liberal, global view. For example, he strongly encouraged the Holy See's relations with the newly-formed United Nations Educational, Scientific and Cultural Organization (UNESCO), joined in this effort by then-Archbishop Angelo Roncalli, the future Pope John XXIII, who had just been appointed Papal Nuncio to France. However, they were overruled by Ottaviani-led forces within the Curia that were wary of diluting any global Church political influence through a multilateral partnership such as UNESCO. This, among a number of other bitter policy disagreements with Ottaviani, resulted in Montini's inglorious dismissal from the Curia in 1954 at Ottaviani's specific behest. The lingering anger between the two would never dissipate, even when Montini was elevated to the papacy as Pope Paul VI.

On January 5, 1955, Montini was sent to become the Archbishop of Milan, which was announced to him in an almost apologetic hour-long phone call from Pope Pius XII himself. However, Montini knew instinctively that the transfer had been orchestrated by Ottaviani. The city of Milan at that time, in the post-World War II period, had become a revolutionary communist bastion, harboring active groups of leftist radicals who were staging violent upheavals throughout Milan and other major urban centers in Italy.

Nonetheless, as soon as he arrived at his new posting, Montini surprised everyone. From the very first day, he became a familiar sight in the city, walking up to workers with a hesitant, nervous smile but always an outstretched hand. Often being greeted by disrespectful hoots and jeers, he persisted in visiting all of the communist districts of the city and going down into mines and touring factories, always carrying a portable kit for saying an impromptu Mass. The new archbishop preached that, irrespective of their differences, "Jesus loves each of us strongly, immensely, divinely," and that the Church would work to satisfy "the profound need for a new and worthwhile life that is hidden in your souls." Gradually he came to be perceived not as a threat but as an empathetic patriarch who was at least willing to listen to their grievances, even if not agreeing with their political beliefs. Although civil unrest continued unabated, it was often more tempered and shorter-lived because Archbishop Montini would personally intervene rather than observe from the sidelines as was the case with his ecclesial predecessors.

Immediately after his election, Pope John had acted to bolster up the depleted numbers in the College of Cardinals. Not only was the Archbishop of Milan the first prelate he elevated to the scarlet, but John thereafter went out of his way to show Giovanni Cardinal Montini special consideration. In 1960, he sent Montini to the United States, where he received an honorary degree from Notre Dame, along with President Eisenhower and the late Dr. Tom Dooley. Afterward, he went on a mission to South America, and in 1962 he made a visit to Africa to report to Pope John on the problems that the Church was facing on that continent.

When Pope John convened Vatican Council II, Montini was the only cardinal from outside of Rome who was invited to stay in one of the papal apartments during the entire eight weeks of the First Session, and he was said to have had a hand in crafting Pope John's historic opening address. Toward the end of the First Session, as it became apparent that no meaningful progress would be made by the time of its recess, Montini sent a letter to his former colleagues in Milan that unequivocally laid the blame for the Council's failures on "the Curial members of the Preparatory Commissions who had prevented cooperation among the various constituencies that laid the groundwork for the Council."

Not surprisingly, news of that letter found its way to the Holy Office – and a furious Cardinal Ottaviani – thus further poisoning an already fractious relationship between the two men.

Murphy was ecstatic. He was seated at the bar toward the entrance of La Carbonara awaiting the arrival of his friend Monsignor Benelli, whose immediate superior had just become the new Pope Paul VI. Murphy couldn't believe his incredible good fortune. Benelli would give him the highest possible Vatican insider access, and he was determined to take full advantage of it.

Cristina was seated next to him on the stool he had reserved for Benelli. She had tables waiting but couldn't pass up this opportunity to sidle up to Murphy, even for a few brief minutes, especially when he was in such an ebullient mood.

"The luck of the Irish, girl! It exists! It does!" he chortled as he gave her an effusive hug. She was surprised but delighted and wrapped her arms around him in return. He then pulled back abruptly when he looked over her shoulder and saw Benelli making his way through the crowded entrance.

He bounced up and embraced his friend. Cristina stood up and Benelli gave her a wink. She laughed, somewhat embarrassed, and then went off to wait on her tables.

"A round of scotches!" called Murphy to the bartender over the din. They sat down on the stools, smiling giddily at each other. Then, as soon as the drinks arrived, they heartily toasted the new pope. They downed the liquor rapidly, slamming the glasses back onto the bar. "Another round!" shouted Murphy. It duly appeared and they were similarly dispatched. A third round arrived but, catching their breath, they now took their time to sip and talk.

"Well?" Murphy asked after a lingering pause, waiting for Benelli to start.

"Well what?" Benelli teased.

"Irish ire can…" Murphy began in a playful burst of anger but was quickly interrupted by Benelli.

"I've just come from His Holiness," Benelli said with a wry smile. "*His Holiness*. I'm going to have to get used to calling him that!" He paused, pursing his lips. "He informed me that I am to continue on with the title 'Principal Aide and Advisor.'"

"Principal Aide and Advisor?" questioned Murphy. "But you were his personal secretary when he was a cardinal. What does that even mean?"

"He said he trusts me," answered Benelli, "so he wants me to be more than just a secretary for him. He wants me to be a *confidante*, to use his word. Not burdened with scheduling and the like."

"Remarkable," said Murphy, turning this news over in his mind. "This is truly remarkable."

"Indeed," replied Benelli. "I still cannot believe it."

"And who is to be his personal secretary?" Murphy asked.

"Someone I don't know well, a Father Pasquale Macchi."

There was a silence as both men let the enormity of the moment sink in. Then Cristina approached and motioned that their table was ready. They downed their scotches, smiled at each other, and followed her into the dining room.

***

Pope Paul was uncertain if he would be able to counter the formidable influence of Cardinal Ottaviani, who had so successfully impeded any meaningful accomplishments during the First Session of Vatican Council II. And that was with *Pope John* on the Throne of St. Peter! Nonetheless, Paul was determined to try. On September 15, 1963, to the surprise of all, he announced the creation of a brand new Steering Commission of four cardinals with an "executive mandate" that would oversee all of the work of the

Second Session. This was clearly intended to thwart any stall tactics by the Ottaviani-led coalition. Three of the Steering Commission's members – Leo Cardinal Suenens of Belgium, Julius Cardinal Dopfner of Germany, and Giacomo Cardinal Lercaro of Italy – were known progressives. The fourth member, Gregorio Cardinal Agagianian of Armenia, although a staunchly conservative member of the Curia, had successfully bridged the gap between the Church of Rome and the Eastern Church (where he was for years the Armenian Patriarch). Paul thus reasoned that he would be open-minded toward at least one of the major issues to be addressed by Vatican Council II, the ambitious long-term goal of reconciliation between the Roman Catholic Church and other Christian faiths.

Pope Paul would therefore not have to take on the "Prophets of Doom" alone.

———

During the week leading up to the opening of the Second Session, Pope Paul scheduled a collective audience for the cardinals in the Curia as well as their top aides. To the surprise of some, who had forgotten this new pope's reputation for punctuality, the pope entered the doorway of the ornate Hall of Benedictions precisely at 10:00 a.m. The majestic room was located near the nave of St. Peter's, above the portico and overlooking the grand piazza fronting the basilica. Its rising fluted Corinthian pilasters supported a vaulted ceiling rich with gold-plated rosettes. It was both awe-inspiring and intimidating – the perfect venue, Pope Paul thought, for the message he was about to deliver.

The pope entered the hall and stiffly walked the length of the room. As he reached his throne on the dais, a few latecomers who had obviously set out at the usual Roman pace for such occasions, slinked to their places toward the empty seats in front while the Holy Father waited impatiently to begin. Cardinal Ottaviani, for his part, had arrived early, trying to gauge in advance a sense of the pending proceedings.

The pope, clearly frustrated at the laggards, calmed himself and began speaking with somber but firm resolve. He reminded them that he knew this audience well, that he had served for thirty years in the ranks of the Vatican Curia. Therefore, he had called this meeting at the beginning of his papacy in order to express to them his personal gratitude for their service. However, he said, there was another reason for this gathering. He wanted to be clear, "*very clear*," that the Curia must fully appreciate the historic importance of Vatican Council II and "*unequivocally support*" its success. "It is my fervent wish, therefore, to be considered as 'the pope who embraced the legacy of John XXIII as his own'... and so shall *you*!"

There were stunned murmurings, exactly as Pope Paul had intended. He then spoke of the necessity for complete accord between the pope and the Curia, putting every single one of them on notice: "There will be *no* efforts from the Curia to disregard the principle wishes of this pope. The Curia is *never* to be suspected of any differences of judgment with regard to decisions of this pope."

Astonished silence followed these harsh words from their historically compliant colleague. Paul continued, "It is understandable that a body such as the Curia, whose present form dates back to 1588, should have grown ponderous with venerable old age, shown by a disparity between its archaic practices and the needs of modern times." This arrow did not miss its mark. "That has made it all the more urgent," he said, "that the Curia should now be 'simplified' and 'decentralized.'" Audible gasps were heard. "People everywhere are watching Rome... *and* the Roman Curia," he noted with escalating intensity. At this, he looked directly at Cardinal Ottaviani and then slowly scanned the others in the room. He finished with a thinly veiled warning, barely disguised as a closing prayer. "This ancient and ever new Roman Curia," he said, pausing, then continuing, "may it now faithfully serve the Church of God in our modern world." After he concluded, he descended from the dais and made his way out of the hall, the only sound the shuffling, soft footsteps of his papal slippers.

"We'll see," Cardinal Ottaviani whispered conspiratorially to Archbishop Parente as they watched the pope exit the hall. "We'll see...."

A week later, Archbishop Parente asked to meet with Cardinal Ottaviani in the conference room of the Holy Office.

"I have disappointing news for Your Eminence," he began, spreading file folders across the highly polished mahogany surface of the century-old conference table. They contained dossiers on every single American bishop who was in attendance at the First Session of the Council. He then handed Cardinal Ottaviani a summary sheet with the following names:

- Patrick Aloysius Boiardi, Bishop of Tulsa
- Fulton J. Sheen, Auxiliary Bishop of New York
- Joseph Maria Grundt, Bishop of New Ulm
- John Francis Dearden, Bishop of Pittsburgh
- Leo Christopher Byrne, Bishop of Wichita
- Lawrence Joseph Shehan, Auxiliary Bishop of New York
- Walter Paul Heston, Bishop of Fargo
- Thomas Joseph Toolen, Bishop of Tucson
- Harold Robert Hoxby, Bishop of Covington
- Robert Emmet Lucey, Bishop of San Antonio
- Albert Gregory Meyer, Bishop of Superior
- William Joseph Brady, Bishop of Manchester
- Joseph Maria Cody, Bishop of Portland
- Thomas Joseph McGucken, Bishop of Sioux City
- Joseph Elmer Ritter, Bishop of St. Louis
- William Edward McManus, Bishop of Fort Wayne-South Bend
- Edward Aloysius Mooney, Bishop of Rochester
- Thomas Joseph Walsh, Bishop of Newark

- William Robert Brady, Bishop of Manchester
- John Baptist Franzoni, Bishop of Youngstown
- Thomas Leo Collins, Bishop of Toledo
- Benjamin Joseph Gumming, Bishop of Fargo
- William Thomas Mulloy, Bishop of Covington
- Joseph Maria Dougherty, Bishop of Buffalo
- Joseph Patrick Hurley, Bishop of St. Augustine
- John Patrick Cody, Auxiliary Bishop of St. Louis
- John Joseph Wright, Bishop of Pittsburgh

"As you know, Your Eminence, over the past weeks I have personally researched the backgrounds of each of these bishops, all of whom will soon be arriving in Rome for the convocation of the Second Session of the Council." He paused, expecting some type of acknowledgement for his extensive efforts, but none was forthcoming.

"Well?" Cardinal Ottaviani followed up impatiently. "Is there a culprit?"

Parente hesitated to provide the following. "Unfortunately, none yet, Your Eminence." He noticed his mentor's scowl. "I will of course do more research upon their arrival for the upcoming session but, I am sorry to say, it may not result in any findings of consequence."

Parente added, "Virtually all of the American bishops played a very passive role in the Council's deliberations, with the notable exception of Joseph Ritter of St. Louis who challenged you publicly during the debate on the sources of divine Revelation."

As Parente expected, Cardinal Ottaviani grimaced angrily at the memory, but he continued. "I therefore spent considerably more time looking into Ritter's background and activities. He is known to be extremely quick tempered and passionate with his progressive viewpoint, possibly explaining his sudden outburst during the Council. However, he was severely chastised afterward by leaders of the American delegation and cautioned to hold his emotions in check or risk jeopardizing any advancement opportunities. Apparently, his ambition took precedence and he issued a lengthy apology to his colleagues, although apparently not to Your Eminence."

"He did *not!*" emphasized Ottaviani.

"I believe Ritter's career aspirations would make him avoid the significant risks associated with being Xavier Rynne," Parente said. He once again paused to gauge Ottaviani's reaction, which was noticeably hostile. He quickly added, "I will of course monitor him closely throughout the upcoming session and..."

"Stop!" Ottaviani interjected loudly. "I must say I am *severely disappointed* in you. I would have expected more." With that, he crumpled up the summary sheet of names and flung it across the conference table at Parente. "Look harder!" he threatened menacingly and swept the file folders in front of him onto the floor. He then stalked out of the conference room, leaving the castigated archbishop alone with the scattered debris.

CHAPTER VII

"It is the *Pauline* Council now!"

The Opening Ceremony of the Second Session of Vatican Council II, on Sunday, September 29, 1963, was impressive, but certainly less formal than the inaugural rites of the First Session. Instead of marching in procession through St. Peter's Square, the leading flank of bishops strolled casually, with mitres in hand, to their tiered seats in the nave of the great basilica. Pope Paul, preceded by the Swiss Guard and the College of Cardinals, was borne aloft on the *sedia gestatoria*, although he dismounted once inside the basilica. Instead of giving those in attendance the customary papal blessing as he walked down the long central aisle, he contented himself with nods and smiles, a humble but well-received gesture. Once he ascended the high altar, Paul made his profession of faith and received the homage of the cardinals. Then, after a solemn Mass, he slowly walked over to the gilded pulpit.

While his opening discourse was unusually long – an hour and four minutes – it would be remembered for its hope and determination, reasserting the purpose of Vatican Council II as envisioned by Pope John and outlining specific steps by which his predecessor's *aggiornamento* would proceed. His voice was somewhat hoarse, but his enunciation was clear and his diction precise. He expressed his profound joy at this reconvening of his religious brethren and fervently prayed that by the time this Council finally concluded its business they "will give their message to the whole world with *one voice alone.*" As he said this, he looked directly at Cardinal Ottaviani, who was now seated among his Curial colleagues in the front row of the congregation instead of on the altar, as he was when Pope John first opened the Council the previous year. Ottaviani stared sternly, defiantly, in return.

Pope Paul then provided a surprisingly honest summary of the shortcomings of the First Session and how he hoped this ten-week Second Session would be more fruitful. He said there *must* be a renewal and reform of the Church, "not by turning upside down the present way of life or breaking with what is essential and worthy in her tradition" – a nod to the conservative coalition – but rather "by stripping it of what is unworthy or defective" – a parallel nod to the progressive wing.

Toward the end of his address, he said that one of the principal aims of Vatican Council II remained taking important first steps toward the reunification of all Christian faiths. He then turned to his left, where the observer-delegates from other Christian communions – Protestant, Eastern Orthodox, and others – were seated. He said their presence at the Council stirred great hope in his heart, as well as a feeling of sadness at their centuries-long separation. "If we are to blame in any way for that separation," he said to them with the utmost sincerity, "we humbly beg God's forgiveness, and ask pardon, too, of our brethren who feel themselves to have been injured by us." This unprecedented apology by a Roman Catholic pontiff shocked many of the assembled clerics, most notably Cardinal Ottaviani, who staunchly held that the Catholic Church was without historic stain or blemish. For many others in the congregation, though, quite possibly a majority, it was an extraordinarily magnanimous moment.

At the end of Paul's discourse, there was silence. However, as he descended from the altar and made his way back down the central aisle, a genuine, slowly escalating applause arose.

The Johannine Council was over. The Pauline Council had begun.

Father Frank Murphy was sitting in the same seat he had occupied during Pope John's memorable address to launch Vatican Council II, in the balcony above the great nave of the basilica. Pope Paul was yet an enigma to him – and to most of those in attendance. He was a veteran of the uncompromising Vatican Curia and yet apparently a progressive determined to move the Church forward. Time would tell what impact he would have on the eventual success of the Council; in particular, how effectively he would deal with those determined to undermine it.

———◆———

The cardinals and bishops gathered together in St. Peter's on Monday morning, September 30, 1963, to begin their deliberations for the Second Session. According to the pre-announced agenda, the first item of business was to be the all-important schema *De Ecclesia*, "On the Nature of the Church." This schema, prepared in advance by Cardinal Ottaviani's Theological Commission, was supposed to incorporate a comprehensive and objective range of proposed changes to Church doctrine covering three main areas, all previously debated during the First Session but with inconclusive results:

- Collegiality – Increasing the role of bishops in advising the pope while diminishing the influence of the powerful Vatican Curia.
- Cultural Diversity – Incorporating local languages and traditions into religious services, instead of the mandatory use of Latin.
- The Diaconate – Expanding the role of deacons to include the ability to baptize, distribute the Eucharist, assist at weddings and bless marriages, bring Holy Communion to the dying, and officiate at funerals and burial services.

Cardinal Ottaviani and his fellow conservatives were vehemently opposed to all three of these proposals. This was reflected in the heavily skewed draft that he now presented to the Council Fathers, directly contravening Pope John's mandate to produce a truly balanced spectrum of opinions.

Not surprisingly, it did not take long for anger to spew forth as more than a dozen delegates rose and trumpeted their alarm that after nine months of work during the interregnum period the Theological Commission's resultant schema completely dismissed even minimal changes to these centuries-old doctrinal policies and practices.

Through it all, Cardinal Ottaviani sat passively, listening almost mindlessly to speaker after speaker, completely unconcerned. Father Murphy, watching carefully from the upper balcony, was as confounded as the rest of the delegates by Ottaviani's unwavering composure.

As the first day of the Second Session came to an end, with weeks of bitter debate on this schema alone sure to follow, Cardinal Ottaviani returned to his office overlooking the piazza fronting St. Peter's. He was met there by Archbishop Parente, who was surprised at his mentor's upbeat mood, considering the hostility of the arguments that had just taken place.

Ottaviani pulled out a dusty bottle of grappa, the potent Italian distilled liquor, and poured two glasses, passing one to Parente. He raised his glass and toasted, "To Lord Salisbury!"

Parente gave him a quizzical look, but raised his glass nonetheless. After a few moments, waiting impatiently for the cardinal to explain, Parente finally asked, "I'm sorry, Your Eminence, but to whom do we toast?"

With a chuckle, clearly uncharacteristic for the curmudgeonly prelate, Ottaviani looked Parente in the eye and explained: "Lord Salisbury was Queen Victoria's last Prime Minister. When an advisor asked him why he didn't object to an excessive spending bill introduced by the opposition, Salisbury laughed and noted that he had tacked on a controversial amendment that would surely lead to endless speechmaking and debate. In the end, without any further intervention on his part, the parliamentary session – along with the unwanted legislation – came to an inconclusive end with no vote taking place. 'And is not that,' Lord Salisbury asked his advisor, 'precisely what we wanted?'"

Parente now understood and nodded with recognition. With only ten weeks allocated for the entire Second Session, the debate on this first schema alone could rage on for weeks, stalling, if not eliminating, any chance for meaningful action on this or any other measure brought before the Council.

Parente let slip a very rare smile. "To Lord Salisbury!" he echoed.

The following weeks did indeed embroil the assembly in demands for a multitude of changes to be incorporated into the schema *De Ecclesia*. And yet, to the surprise of all, with the notable exception of Archbishop Parente, Cardinal Ottaviani remained completely unfazed by the chaotic, acrimonious debate. In fact, he sat politely, contentedly, often smiling, throughout.

———— ◆ ————

Archbishop Parente burst unannounced into Cardinal Ottaviani's office, visibly exhausted but tremendously excited. Ottaviani did not cater to spontaneity; therefore, he was startled at Parente's sudden entrance. However, the cardinal correctly deduced that this must be important. Throughout all the years of working with his second-in-command, he had never witnessed such animated behavior.

"We've got him!" Parente spewed forth, dismissing any formalities and not waiting to be seated. "We've got him!" he repeated. "Xavier Rynne!"

It was now Ottaviani's turn to show excitement, or at least his subdued version of it. Parente did not wait for any acknowledgement or response. He inhaled, trying unsuccessfully to catch his breath, then resumed.

"As you know, Eminence, I did not believe that any of the American cardinals or bishops were capable of authoring *The New Yorker* articles. I therefore began looking for any other Americans who might have been in attendance at the First Session, either as observers or acting as *periti*. The list was somewhat extensive but, after a cursory review of the names, one caught my attention – *Father Francis Xavier Murphy*. His was one of a handful with "Xavier" as either a first, middle or surname. That narrowed the list considerably."

Parente paused once again, still somewhat breathless.

"After researching more deeply into their backgrounds, I soon learned that the maiden name of Murphy's mother was 'Rynne!'"

Cardinal Ottaviani smiled broadly with recognition, albeit in a somewhat ominous way. "Tell me more about him," he spurred Parente.

"He is a Redemptorist priest living at the Accademia Alfonsiana. He arrived in Rome just prior to Pope John's elevation and was asked by an American bishop, Willinger of California, to serve as his *peritus,* thus giving him unlimited access to all of the Council proceedings. He is a published author of theological histories, easily capable of crafting articles of the caliber required for *The New Yorker.* And, according to some of his peers who I spoke with confidentially, he is an unabashed progressive, fully in line with the proposed reforms of the Council."

"Excellent!" Ottaviani crowed. "You have done well, archbishop. *Very* well."

───◆───

Rising on the Council floor later that day, Cardinal Ottaviani exercised his self-conferred prerogative to speak on whatever topic he chose, whenever he chose to do so.

Slowly, audaciously, he approached the microphone in measured steps then cleared his throat.

Instead of addressing any of the ongoing verbal attacks on his *De Ecclesia* draft schema or toward his Theological Commission's allegedly partisan preparatory efforts, he went completely off topic. He immediately launched into an offensive on the *periti* or council experts whom he accused of poisoning the minds of the assembled cardinals and bishops with their radical ideas. He said that he found "no merit in the meddlesome presence of *periti* at this Vatican Council" and he warned that they should be extremely wary of trying to exert undue influence, both within and especially outside of the Council. The latter was a pointed reference to the articles appearing in *The New Yorker* that castigated Cardinal Ottaviani and his fellow members of the Curia. He paused for effect, then, without conclusion, stepped away from the podium and walked pompously back to his seat. After a confused, uncomfortable silence, the debate on *De Ecclesia* resumed.

"What the hell was *that* about?" asked Father Murphy as soon as Monsignor Benelli joined him that evening at a back table at La Carbonara. Benelli was with another Italian priest, in his early forties, whom Murphy did not recognize.

"Well, first let me introduce you to my new colleague, Father Pasquale Macchi," said Benelli. Murphy rose halfheartedly and shook his hand, clearly perturbed at this surprise guest. "He is the personal secretary to our new Pope Paul."

"Ah," Murphy exclaimed, now duly impressed after his standoffish greeting. "It is indeed an honor to make your acquaintance," he enthused.

"As well yours," Macchi responded with lilted but near perfect English. They all sat down and, in a few moments, Cristina arrived to their table.

"Scotch?" inquired Murphy of Macchi.

"Campari and soda."

"Two scotches and a Campari and soda then," Murphy relayed to Cristina, who winked at him, then left with their order.

"And as to your query when we first arrived?" asked Benelli.

"Well, during the debate today, Cardinal Ottaviani rose – out of turn and totally unrelated to the discussion at hand – to complain about *periti* being nuisances at the Council. I am the *peritus* for Bishop Willinger! I felt like it was directed at me!"

Benelli chuckled at Murphy's paranoia. "What have you to worry?" he said. "As you Americans say, 'His sights are set on much bigger fish.'" Both Benelli and Macchi laughed heartily at this clever turn of an American phrase.

Murphy smiled politely but was clearly not placated. Neither Benelli nor his new acquaintance Macchi were aware of his covert relationship with *The New Yorker*. But, he thought, neither was Cardinal Ottaviani, nor anyone else at the Council for that matter. "Maybe I'm making a mountain out of a molehill," Murphy responded, although he was met with confused looks by Benelli and Macchi who did not readily grasp the metaphor.

They paused upon the return of Cristina with their drinks. She smiled flirtatiously at Murphy, which did not go unnoticed by his companions, then left menus and sauntered away to another table.

"Interesting," Macchi whispered to Benelli as he watched Murphy's eyes following Cristina.

"Indeed," responded Benelli.

It was evident that the Second Session of Vatican Council II was in crisis. Just three weeks after convening, a browbeaten malaise had spread among the Council attendees as the debates on *De Ecclesia* droned on; they had already taken up almost a third of the total days allotted for the entire ten-week Second Session. At this pace, with sixteen other proposed schema still on the Council's agenda, one frustrated bishop sarcastically remarked that by the time the last document was presented for debate, the Church would be ready for Vatican Council III.

Alarmed at the seemingly intractable stagnation holding the Second Session hostage, Pope Paul finally took action. On the evening of October 23rd, he called an urgent meeting of his newly created Steering Commission. It included Cardinals Suenens, Dopfner, Lercaro, and

Agagianian as well as the pope's two closest aides, Monsignor Benelli and Father Macchi.

"We are at an impasse," Paul acknowledged, "and we
know the source." He unfairly looked directly at the sole
conservative member of the group, Cardinal Agagianian,
who, nonetheless, nodded his head in agreement with the
others that Cardinal Ottaviani was the culprit.

"We must act. I must act!" Paul said in exasperation. "It
is the *Pauline* Council now!"

"The rules for the debate on *De Ecclesia* are completely
in the favor of the Theological Commission, Your Holiness," responded Cardinal Suenens. "And any proposed
changes must be sent back to the Theological Commission
itself for reevaluation. Only they can prepare a revised
schema for continued debate – and they can do so on their
own schedule."

Pope Paul grumbled. "Cardinal Ottaviani is taking
complete advantage of these rules," he said, stating the
obvious. "And I am sure he had a hand in creating them."
After a pause, Paul continued, visibly agitated. "There will
be nothing accomplished during this Second Session.
Dare I say during this entire Ecumenical Council!"

Paul looked to each of the cardinals in front of him for
some type of reassurance, but none was forthcoming. He
therefore continued, "We must make these 'Prophets of
Doom' understand that they are only a small minority. That
they do NOT reflect the will of the majority at this Council!" His voice continued to rise. "That they do NOT reflect
the will of this *papacy!*" His anger was spewing forth, to the

astonishment – and, quite frankly, relief – of all those present. Pope Paul was finally being spurred into action.

The four cardinals, as well as Benelli and Macchi, shifted nervously in their seats.

"I think I have an idea," the pope finally interjected. "Cardinal Suenens, if you might please stay behind."

"I am confused," Benelli said to Murphy later that night at La Carbonara. "Pope Paul, as you say in America, 'has something up in his sleeve.'"

"Is he going to take on Ottaviani directly?" asked Murphy, ignoring the slight misstep in the wording.

"I am not certain. All I know is that he asked Cardinal Suenens to stay behind, apparently to help plan a memorial Mass for Pope John. But I am certain there was more to that meeting."

"Well, well, the bear has awakened and is emerging from his den," said Murphy, eliciting a laugh from Benelli at this clever – and more understandable – retort. "This will be interesting to see."

The next day the Vatican announced that on the following Monday, October 28th, Pope Paul would say a special Mass to commemorate John XXIII's elevation to the papacy in 1958.

When Monday arrived, St. Peter's was completely filled and the anticipation of the 2,500 gathered prelates was palpable. As Pope Paul walked in, small and slight, almost lost behind the halberds of his guards, the cardinals and bishops suddenly stood up and began to applaud. Surprised by the ovation, the pope was visibly moved. As he ascended the altar and began the introductory prayers before Mass, he lost his place and looked embarrassed. This was unlike his typically serene, always collected, public demeanor. It was the sort of expressive innocence you would have expected from John, but not from Paul, the perfect diplomat always in complete control of himself. However, it further endeared him to his audience.

After a solemn high Mass, Cardinal Suenens, instead of Pope Paul, mounted the imposing gilded pulpit in front of and to the side of the altar. He appeared calm, dignified, and very serious as he put on his glasses and took out his speech. He looked over to the pope, who appeared nervous, then down toward Cardinal Ottaviani, seated with his conservative brethren, who gave him a slightly questioning look in response. An almost imperceptible smile then crossed the corners of Suenens' mouth.

It was immediately evident that Cardinal Suenens was attempting to call forth the spirit of Pope John that had pervaded the opening of Vatican Council II – and to reinvigorate the flagging Second Session of the Council that was now under Pope Paul's purview. He reminded the rapt congregation that many of them had previously regarded Pope John as a merely transitional pope. Yet, as they now well knew, his short-lived papacy had laid the foundation for the Church's historic transition into the modern era. Suenens said that, while it was now the Pauline Council that was upon them, there should be absolutely no doubt that Pope Paul would continue the mandate of Pope John, *aggiornamento*, irrespective of the efforts of those "Prophets of Doom" who would use the power of their offices to hinder the Council's progress. "As you will soon see..."

Spontaneous applause had suddenly erupted throughout the basilica, drowning out Suenens' crucial next lines as he spoke. He looked up and out to the congregation, which only spurred the crescendo. It took a remarkably long time for the assemblage to quiet, at which point Suenens simply disregarded the rest of his speech. What the Council would "soon see" would remain a mystery, but not for long.

As Suenens closed his text and stepped down from the pulpit, another groundswell of applause emerged. Pope Paul himself stood up and added his acclamation. Suenens strode with short steps to the papal altar, bent down and kissed the pope's ring. Then he was warmly embraced by the slim figure in white, to the delight of all those in attendance, except for Cardinal Ottaviani and his cohorts.

At the Council meeting the next morning, Tuesday, October 29th, important new details of Pope Paul's strategy became apparent. Archbishop Pericle Felici, the Presiding Secretary General of the Council, announced that, "By order of His Holiness, printed copies of the schema containing the three points of *De Ecclesia* currently in debate, including all proposed revisions, will be immediately distributed to the Council Fathers for review. Straw votes will then be taken to indicate the general mind of the Council on these important issues and to assist the Theological Commission in its timely review and resubmission of the texts for final approval."

The next day, October 30th, the straw votes were to commence, and a close vote was expected. However, no one thought it would turn out as it did – a landslide calling for incorporating major changes into all three of the schema. The final tally for the first schema concerning Collegiality (giving more power to bishops worldwide and diluting that of the Curia): 1,808 in favor, 336 against. It was an astounding rebuke to Cardinal Ottaviani's Theological Commission.

There were similarly lopsided straw votes in favor of revising the next two schema on Cultural Diversity (incorporating local languages into religious services instead of Latin), and the Diaconate (expanding the role of deacons in the Church).

Was the crisis now over? By ordinary standards, it certainly would have been. However, these straw votes in no way guaranteed that the Council's desired revisions would *actually* be incorporated into the final *De Ecclesia* document. As Cardinal Ottaviani warned immediately after the votes, with so many proposed revisions to the schema it would necessitate "careful, deliberate evaluation" by the Theological Commission. Furthermore, he added, their review could only take place when "due time and consideration could be adequately given."

Recognizing this all-too-obvious stall tactic, Pope Paul sent a terse letter to Cardinal Ottaviani demanding that the Theological Commission meet *immediately* to revise the three *De Ecclesia* schema. Remarkably, Ottaviani flatly refused, informing the pope that because of scheduling conflicts no meeting of the commission could possibly take place for at least a week, if not longer. Separately, Ottaviani quietly advised his commission members that the Council's straw vote was merely a "directive" and "would not be considered binding." Unbeknownst to him, however, a German cleric on the Theological Commission was so appalled by this brazen disregard of the Council's – and the pope's – wishes that he secretly sent a note of concern to the elder statesman of his country's delegation, Josef Cardinal Frings of Cologne.

On the morning of Friday, November 8th, Cardinal Frings rose to speak and publicly called out the subterfuge. "The straw vote of October 30th," he said, "was perfectly clear. I am astonished that Cardinal Ottaviani and the Theological Commission have put this overwhelming vote in doubt. The Theological Commission has no other function but to execute the wishes of, and obey the directives of the Council." He then broadened the target of his denunciation. "This also goes for the Holy Office, whose methods and behavior do not conform at all to the morals and tenets of the modern era. No one should be judged and condemned without having been heard, without knowing what he is accused of, and without having the opportunity to repair what he can reasonably be reproached with."

Frings ended with a bold accusation, "The Holy Office is a cause for scandal in the world!"

Gasps were audible throughout the assembly, and all eyes naturally shifted to Cardinal Ottaviani, who immediately stalked up to the microphone. A nervous hush settled on the gathering. In a voice quaking with rage, Ottaviani shouted, "I most profoundly protest against the accusations made against the Theological Commission and the Congregation of the Holy Office! Without any doubt, it is due to the speaker's utter lack of knowledge. I use this phrase advisedly, so as not to use another that would not be charitable!"

The cardinal's voice was rising in anger. "It is the Theological Commission, and it alone, that is competent here, and not *that* speaker!" he said, pointing his finger directly at Cardinal Frings.

"Furthermore," he continued, "one commits a great mistake in not realizing that the Holy Office is always assured of the help of the most eminent and the most solid men." He pronounced the next sentence slowly and emphatically. "In attacking the Holy Office, one attacks the pope himself as its prefect!" Then he stormed back to his seat.

Without waiting to be recognized, Ernesto Cardinal Ruffini, a fellow conservative, stood up to attack all those who had been criticizing the Roman Curia over the previous weeks. Speaking with similar rage, he said, "I have repeatedly heard in this gathering severe and offensive speeches against the Roman Curia. I say it is unacceptable!"

He went on to confront the elderly Cardinal Frings directly, accusing him of being "out of touch" with what should be required to address such an important, complex issue. "No one other than those with extensive experience in Church matters should even be considered as having an informed opinion," he said.

This sparked cacophonous back-and-forth shouting from the assembled attendees until Archbishop Felici mercifully called an end to the day's debate.

<hr />

That afternoon, Pope Paul acceded to an urgent request by Cardinal Ottaviani for an audience. He was accompanied by Ildebrando Cardinal Antoniutti, Prefect of the Congregation for Religious, the Curia department that oversaw all matters affecting priests, as well as by Ottaviani's close colleague Cardinal Siri.

After a cursory and intentionally disrespectful, half-hearted nod toward Pope Paul, Cardinal Ottaviani started right in, not even waiting for his colleagues to be seated.

"Holy Father," he began abruptly, "I must say that I am *outraged* at the behavior of certain cardinals during the deliberations in the Council this morning." He paused, looking for acknowledgement from Pope Paul but receiving none, clearly blind to the irony of his statement. He inhaled slowly in a vain attempt to calm himself, then continued. "Accusations were made, without merit, about the work of the Theological Commission, including personal attacks against certain of its members." Pope Paul tried to suppress a subtle smile, but it was caught by Ottaviani. "You do not take this matter seriously?" he challenged.

"Of course I do, Your Eminence," Paul responded with a bit more control over his countenance. "Please continue."

"The stakes for our Holy Mother Church...for keeping at bay forces of...for heinous mistakes that..." Ottaviani stammered, not able to complete his thoughts, losing his composure. "...And the outrageous lies that are being aired!"

Pope Paul had never seen Ottaviani like this; neither had Cardinals Antoniutti and Siri. When Ottaviani surprisingly did not resume his tirade, Paul calmly responded, "Sometimes when we open a window, the stale air is replaced by a fresh, invigorating breeze."

The biting metaphor was not lost on Ottaviani and infuriated him even further. Antoniutti and Siri stood motionless, clearly not willing to engage in the confrontation.

"Must I therefore assume, Your Holiness, that you will actually *tolerate* such egregious behavior?"

"Egregious, no. Long overdue, yes."

Ottaviani, shocked, paused to carefully consider his next words. "If that is the case, Holy Father, it may be necessary for me to resign."

Paul raised his hand and cut him off. "Stop. I know you well, my dear cardinal, and I know that such a threat is idle." He waited for Ottaviani to interject, but he did not, so Paul continued. "It is my understanding that you made a similar threat to Pope John during the First Session when you also complained about criticism from the Council Fathers."

That was indeed the case. When the Council Fathers in that session were presented with the schema on the sources of divine Revelation, prepared by Cardinal Ottaviani's Theological Commission with a dramatically skewed bias, there was a nearly universal outcry denouncing his complete dismissal of the delegates' extensive input.

Ottaviani had then called on Pope John to protest their caustic dissension. "If this goes on much longer, the dignity of those in the Holy Office will be in danger, and I may be compelled to resign!" he warned.

Pope John replied without hesitation, "No you will not. Power is intoxicating, Your Eminence, and in that regard you are well sated. As for your dignity, however, I have no assurance." Ottaviani stormed out of Pope John's office, furious, although never relinquishing his role.

Now, one year later, in an equally heated circumstance, Cardinal Ottaviani was again being rebuffed by a surprisingly resilient pope.

Father Murphy was in an exceptional mood. His most recent articles had been enthusiastically received by *The New Yorker* and, as his editor Bill Shawn relayed, the impact of Xavier Rynne's "Letter from Vatican City" series had been nothing short of extraordinary. Shawn pressed him for the next installment, which Murphy promised would be forthcoming. "As you will see," Murphy said, "there is a colossal tug-of-war taking place between Pope Paul and

Cardinal Ottaviani, with the future of the Catholic Church at stake – and no clear winner in sight!"

After they hung up, Murphy began to write a detailed summary of the first half of the Second Session. As he did so, he simply had to vent:

> The Theological Commission, in charge of rewriting schema, meets only when it is summoned by Cardinal Ottaviani, and he has seen fit to convene it only once a week, if then....
>
> Many of the Council Fathers realize that Cardinal Ottaviani does not regard the daily debates in St. Peter's as having any legislative force whatsoever. If the Theological Commission is free to follow or dismiss the Council Fathers' wishes at its own discretion, what guarantee is there that the true will of the Council will ever be expressed....
>
> Cardinal Frings of Cologne, echoing the sentiment of many of the Council Fathers, said, "The Holy Office, headed by Cardinal Ottaviani, whose methods and behavior do not conform at all to the modern era, are a source of harm to the faithful and a cause of scandal to the world....[5]

Murphy then continued with a more straightforward accounting of the Second Session's early proceedings, but knew he was going to be hard-pressed going forward to keep his escalating anger in check.

---

[5] "Letter from Vatican City," *The New Yorker*, November 30, 1963

About a week later, Murphy received a strange request from Monsignor Benelli to meet with him and Father Macchi at a restaurant in the Piazza del Popolo, one of Rome's most beautiful squares but located far away from the Vatican and the usual tourist haunts. Its massive elliptical pedestrian space, ornate fountains, dominant central obelisk, and historic arches marking the ancient entryway to Rome, all combined to make it a favorite among locals. Interestingly, for centuries it was also the primary site for staging Roman executions.

As Murphy crossed the Tiber on the Ponte Margherita, he spotted Benelli and Macchi standing between the two nearly identical basilicas fronting the piazza, Santa Maria in Montesanto and Santa Maria dei Miracoli. He waved to them but only received half-hearted acknowledgements in return.

"Thank you for coming, my dear friend," said Benelli as they all shook hands somewhat formally then crossed to Rosati, a secluded artistic and literary café nearby. "Let us dine inside."

Given the beautiful evening and available outdoor seating, this caught Murphy by surprise. He followed them through the front door and then, although there were more empty tables in the main dining room, they ascended a back stairway to the second level. While the view of the bustling piazza below was especially remarkable, their seclusion from the rest of the patrons was disarming.

Once seated, a waiter arrived and they placed an order for wine and antipasti. As soon as he left, Father Macchi began in earnest.

"Remember a few weeks ago when you were worried that Cardinal Ottaviani might have singled you out during a speech?" he asked.

"Yes, and I am still concerned," responded Murphy uneasily.

"Well, there *was* a reason…that I am sure I should not divulge…but it may be important for your personal wellbeing," Macchi said.

"Personal wellbeing?" queried Murphy at hearing this unexpected, and certainly upsetting, choice of words. He looked to Benelli, who apparently knew where this conversation was going.

"Last night I saw a letter on a sideboard in the office of His Holiness," Macchi said, almost in a whisper, extremely conflicted about what he was about to divulge. "I feel compelled to pass it along to you…actually my translation of the letter into English. I transcribed it rapidly while I was alone in his office."

"And what did it say?" nudged a clearly worried Murphy.

Macchi took out a wrinkled piece of paper from his inside jacket pocket. On it was his hurriedly handwritten transcription from Italian to English of a letter from Cardinal Ottaviani to Archbishop Felici, the Council's Secretary General. It read as follows:

Palace of the Holy Office

Most Reverend Eminence,

Certainly it has not escaped your most reverend Excellence the article with the signature Xavier Rynne published in the widespread American weekly *The New Yorker*. In it the author spreads criticisms in a manner most questionable and partisan in regard to determined Council Fathers of the Roman Curia and in particular of the Holy Office.

According to the opinion of qualified persons, the signature of Xavier Rynne appears similar to that of the Redemptorist Father Francis Xavier Murphy, whose mother's name is Rynne.

May your Excellency see whether it might not be opportune to call the attention of the Rector Major of the Redemptorists to this matter in order to have him forbid Father Murphy to write articles of this kind and to take appropriate disciplinary action.

May I profit by this occasion to express my sincere esteem,

For your Most Reverend Excellency
Alfredo card. Ottaviani, segr.

Murphy read the letter with shock. As soon as he finished, Macchi passed him a second piece of paper, with a similarly hurried transcription from Italian to English.

Vatican City

Most Reverend Eminence,

With reference to the venerable letter of your most reverend Eminence, in which your Eminence signals an article of Francis Xavier Murphy, published in the American weekly *The New Yorker* in which the author criticizes certain conciliar Fathers and the Roman Curia, and in particular the Holy Office, allow me to inform you that I have already spoken of the matter with the Holy Father, who has assured me that he will take the necessary measures.

May I take this occasion to renew to your Eminence my profound esteem.

Your Most Reverend
Pericle Felici, seg.gen.

"And these were in Pope Paul's personal office?" Murphy asked. "So the pope is aware?"

Macchi nodded.

"Dear God," Murphy mumbled. *"Dear... God."*

———— ••• ————

During the rapidly dissipating last weeks of the Second Session, close to a dozen of the scheduled schema were hastily presented for consideration by the Council Fathers.

However, as heated discussions regarding proposed revisions devolved into protracted verbal quagmires, debates were artificially cut short in the hopes that at least some of the remaining schema might be salvaged. Unfortunately, this did not occur and it became painfully obvious that the insidious efforts of Cardinal Ottaviani and his Curial cohorts to sabotage the Second Session had indeed been successful.

Only one decree, albeit an important one, was pushed through on the very last day of the session: approval for religious services to finally be celebrated in the local language of congregations (a subsection of *De Ecclesia*). However, the failure to bring any other schema to a final vote far outweighed this singular achievement.

On Wednesday, December 4th, 1963, the Second Session of Vatican Council II officially came to what virtually all observers regarded as a truly inglorious end. The entrance of Pope Paul into St. Peter's for the final solemn ceremony was dignified but sedate. Similar to the opening ceremony of the Second Session, the pope was preceded by the full panoply of the papal household and liveried guards, the Eastern patriarchs, and the College of Cardinals robed in white copes and mitres. Then Pope Paul himself appeared, this time carried high on the *sedia gestatoria* the entire length of the long, central nave, a poorly received symbolic attempt on his part to reinforce his papal prestige. As he proceeded, he scarcely looked to the right or left to acknowledge the fitful applause from the benches.

As the *sedia gestatoria* was lowered at the base of the high altar, Pope Paul alighted and mounted the steps leading to the papal throne. There he was met by Eugene Cardinal Tisserant, the eighty-year-old stand-in for Cardinal Ottaviani, who had informed the pope that he once again preferred to "sit among my colleagues." Cardinal Tisserant offered an opening prayer in poorly enunciated Latin, which was answered by the congregation with rote precision and dispatch. A formal Mass then followed, after which Pope Paul rose to begin his address to officially close the Second Session of Vatican Council II.

In a carefully worded summation, the pope stressed the spiritual rather than any literal successes of the Second Session. He insisted that it had given the gathered prelates from around the world an unprecedented camaraderie with each other and thereby enabled them to experience the significance of St. Paul's words as quoted in Ephesians 2:19-20: "You are no longer strangers and newcomers, but rather fellow citizens of the saints and members of the household of God."

However, fully sensitive to the widespread criticisms of the Second Session, Pope Paul admitted that the discussions over the preceding ten weeks had been "arduous" and he referred to the work of the Council Fathers as "unfortunately laborious." Yet, he said, it was because of these challenges that it was more important than ever to continue with the mission of Vatican Council II, as outlined by Pope John in his historic call to action. "We hope that the Third Session in the autumn of next year will bring the discussions to completion," he concluded.

To the amazement of some, to the consternation of others, Vatican Council II would continue.

CHAPTER VIII

———— ●◄ ————

"We will change everything back to the way it was!"

O n the afternoon of December 4th, 1963, mere hours after the official closing of the Second Session of Vatican Council II, Pope Paul met secretly with the three observer delegates from the Eastern Orthodox Church: Maximos IV Saigh, the Greek Melkite Catholic Patriarch of Antioch; Meliton of Chalcedon, the Metropolitan of the Greek Orthodox Church of Chalcedon; and Paul of Finland, the Metropolitan of the Greek Orthodox Metropolis of Finland. Also present was the pope's personal secretary, Father Pasquale Macchi.

Pope Paul reminded them of his speech to open the Second Session that a principal aim of Vatican Council II was to begin the process of eventual reunification with all Christian faiths. While their attendance at the Council was an important symbolic gesture toward that goal, he said, as was the presence of representatives from other Christian denominations (Anglican, Lutheran, Presbyterian, Reformed), the pope insisted something more concrete was now needed.

For the Eastern Orthodox, their separation from the Catholic Church dated from the East-West Schism in 1054. That split resulted from a combination of factors, including Eastern Orthodox resistance against papal authority, phrasing in the Nicene Creed regarding the Holy Spirit, and even the type of bread used in the Eucharist (leavened for Eastern Orthodox, unleavened for Roman Catholic).

Pope Paul took from his desk two letters. Both were from Patriarch Athenagoras I of Constantinople, the *primus inter pares* or "first among equals" of all Orthodox patriarchs, who was not in attendance at the Council. The first letter, dated June 22, 1963, congratulated Paul on his ascendancy to the papacy. The second letter, dated November 22, 1963, offered Athenagoras' support and prayers for the beleaguered pontiff as the difficult Second Session was grinding inconclusively to its end.

"I was deeply moved by both letters, especially the second," the pope said with emotion as he passed them over. "I thought they might signal an opportunity for us to take a first step together." He then nodded toward Father Macchi, who continued.

"I have just returned from a special errand for His Holiness," Macchi began. "In the strictest secrecy I traveled to the Holy Land to prepare the groundwork for a possible pilgrimage by the pontiff – hopefully together with Patriarch Athenagoras – at the beginning of the new year."

The three delegates looked with surprise at the pope, then uncertainly at each other.

"I would ask if you could pass a request on to Patriarch Athenagoras on my behalf," said Pope Paul.

All three hesitated, but nodded politely, then took their leave.

It was the briefest of papal excursions but one of the most historic. Pope Paul landed in Jerusalem on January 4th, 1964; Patriarch Athenagoras arrived a few hours later. They each toured some of the holiest sites in Christendom over the next day and half before coming together at the residence of Patriarch Benedict of Jerusalem on January 6th.

"The Christian world has lived for centuries in the night of separation. Its eyes are tired of gazing into darkness," said Athenagoras in his formal greeting. "May this meeting be the dawn of a bright and blessed day in which future generations, communicating from the same chalice of the sacred body and precious blood of the Lord, praise and glorify, in charity, peace and humility, the one Lord and Savior of the world."

In a wonderful coincidence, Pope Paul had actually brought with him a gold chalice as his personal gift to the patriarch for the occasion. He presented the chalice to Athenagoras, saying, "As you just mentioned in your welcome, let this chalice be a symbol of the hoped-for restoration of fraternal communion between our two Churches."

Athenagoras followed with his gift to Pope Paul, a pectoral chain – an *encolpion* in the Greek Church – a sacred emblem worn by its bishops. The significance was powerful; he was recognizing Pope Paul as a fellow bishop of the Eastern Church.

The pope's eyes lit up when he saw what it was; he knew what it represented. At once, without hesitation, he removed his Latin papal stole and put the pectoral chain over his head. Then, with the assistance of the patriarch, he put the papal stole back on. "Now let us together read the Gospel of St. John, chapter 17, the prayer of Christ for unity," he offered.

As prearranged, a special New Testament volume with the Latin and Greek texts facing each other was held up between them. The pope began with a verse in Latin and was followed by the patriarch with the next verse in Greek. Pope Paul was so overcome by emotion that he lost his place at least three times.

The final words of the passage, "Let them be one so that the world may believe," were enunciated by the pope with particular emphasis. They then recited the "Our Father" in unison. Athenagoras at first hesitated to go beyond the words with which the Latin version customarily ended, but the pope insisted, and they both said together the concluding phrase, which the Orthodox say along with

Protestants: "For thine is the kingdom, the power, and the glory forever. Amen."

Upon his return to Rome, the pontiff was accused by some critics of political stagecraft to offset the failures of the Second Session. But none could deny the compelling symbolism of two of the most important religious leaders in the world coming together to begin the process of reconciliation in the birthplace of Christianity itself.

The decree passed at the end of the Second Session that allowed for the incorporation of local languages into religious services was in trouble. According to the final text approved by the Council Fathers, the timing of its implementation was to be at the sole discretion of cardinals and bishops in their respective dioceses. However, there remained a powerful group of cardinals within the Curia who were still livid at its passage and had not given up on the Latin mandate.

The Curia's Congregation of Rites was the Vatican department in charge of the document's promulgation. It was led by Giacomo Cardinal Lercaro, a close confidante of Cardinal Ottaviani. Incredibly, his congregation took it upon itself to secretly alter a key sentence in the final draft, unbeknownst to the Council Fathers, requiring that any liturgical changes made from Latin into a vernacular language must be approved by the Holy See, i.e., the Vatican Curia.

Once this subterfuge was discovered, an ecclesiastical firestorm erupted. It was led by German, French, and Belgian bishops who simply ignored the doctored text and forged ahead with local translations in their respective countries. Pope Paul was similarly shocked by the brazenness of Cardinal Lercaro and the congregation's unilateral, unauthorized action. He immediately decreed that only the original text approved by the Council Fathers would be sanctioned with papal authority.

As Pope Paul subsequently learned, Paolo Cardinal Marella, one of the most conservative cardinals in the Curia, had earlier bragged to his colleagues, "Have no fear. Once the talk ceases and the bishops depart, we will change everything back to the way it was!"

It was clearly not an idle threat.

Frank Murphy's royalty checks from *The New Yorker* had been accumulating in his desk drawer, and they were much larger than he could have ever anticipated. The very first was accompanied with a simple, one-word handwritten note: "Enjoy!" He certainly intended to do so. His first thought? To celebrate grandly with Cristina. Therefore, one night he walked jauntily to La Carbonara to seek her out, although as he neared the restaurant he became unaccustomedly nervous. Their relationship, while growing in closeness, had never extended beyond the confines of her workplace. He was hoping that would change.

As he entered the restaurant there were a number of open stools at the bar, and Murphy took an isolated one at the end. Cristina, in the dining area, saw him enter, smiled and winked, then continued taking an order from a young couple. Murphy smiled back, unintentionally wanly, and turned to the bartender to order a scotch. Cristina went to the kitchen, entered the table's order, then sauntered happily toward Murphy, giving him a warm, lingering embrace.

"How are you this evening, Frank?" she whispered into his ear, clearly overjoyed to see him alone.

"Excellent now that I am here with you!" he replied flirtatiously, with the desired effect on Cristina. "Can you sit and talk for a bit?"

Scanning the nearly empty restaurant, she replied, "Of course!"

Murphy's scotch arrived and he downed it rapidly, somewhat alarming Cristina, who was trying to gauge its meaning. He immediately signaled for another, then paused until it was promptly delivered. It was likewise quickly consumed and he ordered a third.

"Are you okay?" she asked concerned.

"Actually, never better," he said, the warmth of the scotches now taking hold. He looked directly into her eyes. "Never better, Cristina," he repeated, much more confidently. She smiled, relieved, and he broadened his grin. He took her hand in both of his, which seemed completely natural. They each looked down at their clasped hands, then up at each other: she smiling nervously, he now more self-assured.

"When is the next evening that you are free?" he asked.

She paused, but barely. "Wednesday."

"Grand," Murphy responded. "Let me treat you to a wonderful dinner. Somewhere away from here," he said, motioning with a sweeping gesture. Her eyes welled with a hint of tears.

"Yes, yes," she said. "I would love that." They stared at each other, suddenly a bit awkwardly, neither one speaking. Both of them now seemed a bit conflicted at the reality of their relationship moving on to a new level.

"My table..." Cristina finally said, slightly embarrassed, taking her hand out of his and returning to work.

Luciana had invited Murphy to lunch at the oldest café in Rome, Antico Caffè Greco, at the base of the Spanish Steps. Despite its location, it was rarely frequented by tourists but rather by a very sophisticated clientele for whom price was not a concern. The narrow, richly ornate interior was adorned with centuries-old paintings and sculptures, interspersed with black-and-white photographs of artists, writers, and social elites who had frequented there. Luciana, in her fashionable heels, designer skirt, and sheer white blouse was easily the most beautiful woman in the café – and she looked right at home.

Murphy placidly kissed her hand then sat down in the seat across from her. She gazed at him for a few minutes, noticing a subtle distraction in his demeanor. Unable to pinpoint her uncertainty just yet, she inquired casually as to his wellbeing.

"I am wonderful, Luciana," he said almost absent-mindedly.

She had expected a compliment from him, as was his usual habit upon first seeing her, or even a bit of flirtation. But none came forth. Her intuition was pricked. A waiter appeared and she ordered a Campari and soda; he ordered the same. Murphy began glancing around at the many wall coverings, certainly not focusing on Luciana, his thoughts elsewhere. She reached out her hand to touch his, regaining his attention.

Casual but disappointing, non-descript conversation followed over a light lunch. Then, as the meal was nearly complete, Luciana inquired if anything was on his mind.

"Nothing at all, Luciana, nothing at all."

She didn't press him further. And she didn't address the real reason for her invitation, to urge his increasing involvement with the orphanage at Villa Nazareth. Something was different. Amiss? As soon as the check arrived, he stood and thanked her, kissed her politely on the cheek, and disappeared outside into the crowd.

<hr />

"**Absolutely NOTHING!**" Cardinal Ottaviani blared to Archbishop Parente. "They have done ABSOLUTELY

NOTHING!" His fury was directed toward the absence of any type of disciplinary follow-through regarding Xavier Rynne's articles in *The New Yorker*.

"With deference, Your Eminence, Father Murphy has been brought to the attention of the pontiff himself," said Parente.

This only angered the cardinal further. "Well, *he* certainly won't take action on *my* behalf," Ottaviani glowered. "Did not that priest take the Oath of Secrecy for these Council proceedings? Did not we all?" he questioned.

Parente nodded, knowing full well the answer. As did Ottaviani.

"It is apostasy, I say! Heresy!"

A dangerous accusation, thought Parente, although he did not dare share this concern with the cardinal in his current temperament. *Was he contemplating excommunication?*

"We will have to pursue this matter ourselves," Ottaviani hissed.

"I have a favor to ask of you," Murphy said to his fellow Redemptorist, the Italian André Sampers, whose room was down the hall from his own at the Accademia Alfonsiana.

"Anything," Sampers readily answered, still somewhat awestruck with his American friend, although he had seen little of him in recent months, except in passing.

Murphy hesitated, uncertain how to broach his question. "Well, my friend, it looks like I may be coming into some more money."

"That is wonderful," Sampers replied. "I am happy for you." Then he caught himself. "Unless of course it means that a loved one has passed away."

"No, no... nothing like that," Murphy responded. Then he hesitated again. "But I have received some checks... and I am a bit uncomfortable placing them in my existing accounts."

Sampers looked at him curiously, but Murphy could not explain that he was trying to somehow distance himself from any monies directly tied to *The New Yorker*.

Murphy continued, "André, I know you have many contacts... and possibly some in banking?"

Sampers offered, "If you need to cash a check, there are many places here in Rome that can accommodate you."

That was clearly not what Murphy required so he had no choice but to throw caution to the wind. "André, is it possible to have a bank account that would not be readily associated with me?" He paused, gauging Sampers' reaction, which was guarded but not antagonistic. "There is nothing untoward about these checks," Murphy clarified. "It's just that, well, I don't want questions to be raised when there is no need."

Sampers thought for a moment, putting his hand to his chin, contemplating the various aspects of this unusual request.

Murphy held his breath, uncertain if he had crossed a line. Agonizing seconds passed. Then, hesitatingly, Sampers half-heartedly responded, "Okay."

Visibly relieved, Murphy went to his room, retrieved the checks from *The New Yorker*, and brought them back to Sampers.

"I will see what I can do," Sampers said, taking note of the remitter of the checks.

"Thank you, André," Murphy responded. "Indeed, you are a true friend."

———◆———

Murphy waited for Cristina at Mirabelle, the trendy rooftop terrace restaurant of the Hotel Splendide Royale. He was dressed in casual street clothes rather than his clerical garb: a white oxford shirt underneath a lightweight navy blue dinner jacket, gray slacks, penny loafers. The terrace offered spectacular views of Rome, with the dome of St. Peter's proudly visible in the distance. The evening was perfect; the sky streaming from reddish pink to darkening blue with a subtle, cooling breeze. Murphy had never been to Mirabelle before but had heard that it was a favorite of foreign diplomats eager to impress their visiting colleagues. It was also "romantic as hell," as one American journalist quipped sarcastically to Murphy, oblivious to his intentions.

Cristina exited her taxi at the hotel entrance. She was greeted by a footman wearing a top hat and cape who opened a heavy glass door for her. As she entered, she was struck by the richly ornate lobby with its gold leaf ceiling rosettes and massive mirrors along each wall reflecting light from multiple crystal chandeliers. To the left were a series of frightening paintings of ancient cardinals and popes, all seemingly looking down upon her with judgment. She was feeling overwhelmed; whatever confidence she had nurtured throughout the day was diminishing rapidly. She took a deep breath, composed herself, and located the elevators. She crossed the lobby and waited, taking another deep breath before pressing the button. With the *ding* of the elevator, a group of exuberant tourists spilled out. She entered, alone, nervous.

The ambiance as the elevator door opened onto the terrace was breathtaking. Beyond the white linen, candle-lit tables with fresh floral arrangements was an expansive view of the city of Rome she had never experienced. As she stepped out, more than a few men looked up and glanced in her direction, smiling admiringly. She slowly scanned the terrace, finding Murphy standing up at a table in the far corner. She smiled and walked gingerly over to meet him, trying desperately to look poised. She was dressed in a fitted dark blue skirt with black pumps and a flowing, multicolored silk blouse. Her hair was pulled back in an elegant chignon. When she reached the table, Murphy took her hands in his. "You look beautiful, Cristina," he said with obvious joy. He gave her a kiss on the cheek and then pulled out the chair next to his. Before sitting, she took a moment to once again admire the remarkable panorama, something she would not soon forget. It was exactly the first impression Murphy had intended.

An extraordinary traditional Italian five-course meal followed, with their gasps of delight greeting every new offering. The conversation and wine flowed freely and, as the sun gradually set, the lights of the Eternal City came to life. For both of them, the evening ended all too soon; as it was, they were among the last of the patrons to leave. Reluctantly, they took the elevator down to the hotel lobby, where they lingered among the magnificent, gilded appointments. Murphy then led her by the arm to the front entrance where a line of taxis awaited.

"This was such a wonderful evening, Frank," she demurred. "How can I thank you enough?"

"The pleasure was all mine," he responded. He kissed her, fully on the lips. She responded warmly, naturally, unhesitatingly. Then she stepped back, turned, and entered an awaiting taxi. She looked out the window and waved at Murphy, who was smiling wistfully, almost imperceptibly, as the taxi sped off.

<hr />

"**What do you mean?**" Luciana asked, clearly confused by the information being given to her over the telephone.

"It is a new bank account that was just opened," the gravelly male voice repeated, "on behalf of your acquaintance, Father Murphy." He paused, then added, "A Redemptorist priest here in Rome made an unusual request with certain provisos for…well…discretion." He waited on the line for a response from her but there was only silence.

"Is there something else?" Luciana finally asked impatiently.

The voice on the other end of the line hesitated.

"Well?" she pursued, slightly irritated.

"He has met someone," the voice said. "His interests, his priorities may…" He paused, then felt compelled to ask, "Are you sure he is still willing to help us?"

Luciana thought for a few seconds, then responded, "Yes, yes…I am sure it will all be fine." She thanked him for the information and, after a few courtesy inquiries about the caller's family, hung up the phone.

She immediately called Frank Murphy and invited him to come to her home the next afternoon for a visit. Initially he wavered, but then, to her relief, he accepted. She lived in Villa Borghese, one of the quieter but certainly among the most upscale neighborhoods in all of Rome. Hers was one of the few stand-alone villas tucked in among stately townhouses and elegant apartments. It was directly across from one of the most beautiful parks in Rome, Villa Borghese, from which the neighborhood took its name. Covering more than eighty hectares, the park was a peaceful oasis from the hustle and bustle of the city, dotted throughout with statuary, fountains, and scenic pathways.

The next day as his taxi arrived, Murphy could not have been more impressed. Luciana's villa had a timeless, Mediterranean allure. Its exterior stucco walls were punctuated with ivy and bougainvillea climbing gracefully up the façade, and its terracotta-tiled roof was crowned with weathered clay tiles. A wrought-iron gate, adorned with intricate patterns, opened into a small cobblestone court-yard where she sat, awaiting him.

As usual, she looked stunning. She wore a knee-length, powder-blue dress with a subtle sheen that caught the slanted rays of the early afternoon sun. A simple pair of pearl earrings and a matching pearl necklace was the only jewelry she wore. Oversized, cat-eye sunglasses were perched on top of her head. Surprisingly, she wore flats instead of her usual high heels.

"Let us go for a walk," she said, "to delight in this beautiful day together." She put her arm in his and they crossed the street to enter the park. They walked silently for a few minutes, the only sound the billowing of her skirt swaying with her slow, graceful movements.

"I want to tell you a story," she soon began as they continued walking. "It is time."

Murphy was intrigued.

"I grew up in a very small village in Lombardy, Tirano, in the northern part of Italy, only two kilometers from the border with Switzerland. In 1939, before Italy entered World War II, our train station saw many movements of Swiss soldiers enjoying their leave in our local cafés and bars. At the time I was sixteen years old, somewhat rebellious, and, quite honestly, very beautiful."

Murphy smiled at the obviousness of her remark but remained silent.

"On many nights my friends and I would gather to enjoy their company – flirting, dancing, receiving free drinks. However, one night I met an extremely handsome Swiss soldier and … ashamedly … well … became pregnant."

Murphy held his shock in check.

"Before dishonor could be brought upon my family, my father sent me away, to the Benedictine Convent of St. John at Mustair, in the southeastern part of Switzerland. While there, my pregnancy progressed. However, when it came time to give birth, there were no doctors available because of the pressing needs of the military. The sisters did the best they could, but there were complications. My child did not survive, and almost neither did I. It took months for me to recover. Unfortunately, however, as a result of the difficult birth, I became sterile.

"The Swiss soldier who I had slept with returned periodically looking for me. On one of his visits, a friend of mine recognized him and told him of my situation. Although he became aware of my location, he did not visit. His father, however, in apparent guilt for his son's transgression, sent an extremely generous donation to the convent.

"When I had regained my health, the good sisters bade me farewell but also gave me the entirety of the donation. I thanked them and traveled to the remote village of Chur in the Swiss Alps, where I remained until the Italian surrender.

"I refused to return to my family, so I chose Rome because it was the opposite of Tirano – a large city where I

THE MOLE OF VATICAN COUNCIL II

was not known and far away from the shame of my past. I began my life anew. With my Swiss Francs extremely valuable compared to the post-war Lira, I was able to support not only myself but also provide opportunities for many people and businesses to rebuild. It proved to be very lucrative."

Luciana paused, and then confessed, "But I was lonely. Then one day I was approached by Cardinal Tardini, who had heard of my largesse and was seeking support for his struggling orphanage, Villa Nazareth. I, of course, obliged. And with his help I was able to adopt my beloved son, Fabrizio, who is now in his studies at university in London."

To Murphy's surprise, they had suddenly ended up at the same entrance to the park from which they had embarked. He had not said a word on their walk. He looked up to see Luciana's villa, now with her car and driver parked out front. They crossed the street and the car door was opened for him.

She kissed him softly on the lips, then stepped back as he entered the car. As he looked out the window at her, she seemed shaken, vulnerable. He had never seen her so. She turned and walked back into her courtyard as the car sped away into the bustling traffic.

***

In anticipation of the Third Session of Vatican Council II, now only a few weeks away, Murphy submitted his next article to *The New Yorker*, explaining in detail not only the many crucial issues yet to be addressed but also concluding with his deep concerns about the insurgent Curial efforts to undermine any meaningful progress by the Council:

> As the Council Fathers converge on St. Peter's from all over the world for the inauguration of the Third Session of Vatican Council II, observers here are speculating on whether the reform and renewal of the Church will be advanced or stifled....
>
> There is a fear that the obstructionist tactics adopted by the conservative minority during the session last fall will once again be employed....
>
> Paul VI's conflicts with Cardinal Ottaviani have unfortunately reawakened memories of the excesses of the Holy Office earlier in this century. The tactics of the heresy-hunters of that era were as un-Christian as the heresy itself. Those zealots were motivated not by a love of truth but by personal vindictiveness and hatred....[6]

Summer was at an end and Rome was slowly beginning to fill once again with the cacophony of Church officials from around the world in anticipation of the upcoming Third Session. Murphy's own world was soon to become considerably busier, but for now there was one last weekend all to

---

[6]"Letter from Vatican City," *The New Yorker,* September 19, 1964

himself…and Cristina. Murphy asked her if she would like to return to the site of their previous dinner together, the rooftop terrace restaurant Mirabelle. She was, of course, thrilled.

He made the reservation and, as expected, the setting and dinner were once again spectacular. However, as the meal ended and the check arrived, all too soon for both of them, Murphy suddenly became nervous, completely out of character from his demeanor earlier in the evening.

"What is it, Frank?" Cristina asked. "Is there something wrong?"

He simply looked at her and said, "Of course not. This evening, this whole summer, has been truly wonderful. I just don't want it to end."

She laughed, relieved. "Neither do I," she demurred.

He smiled, then hesitated again, finally speaking up, "I *truly* do not want it to end."

Cristina looked at him curiously, uncertain how to respond.

Murphy was becoming uncomfortable now. Had he said too much? Was he moving too fast?

Finally, he inhaled and reached for her hand. She clasped his in return. They stood and walked slowly to the elevator. Once it arrived, Murphy pressed a button, but it was for a middle floor of the hotel itself. She noticed. Soon enough, the door opened and Murphy stepped out, turned with his arm outstretched, and waited. Cristina, surprised and clearly flustered, with tears beginning to form, hesitated. Then she reached down and pushed the button for the lobby, the elevator doors closing between them.

CHAPTER IX

———◆———

"*Magno cum dolore* – With great pain"

The stakes could not have been higher for the Third Session of Vatican Council II, set to commence on September 14, 1964. Once again, cardinals and bishops from around the world were being summoned to Rome for ten weeks to fulfill Pope John's promise of *aggiornamento*, bringing the Catholic Church up-to-date in the modern world.

By all accounts, Pope Paul, as his successor, had failed miserably.

By contrast, the conservative coalition, led by Alfredo Cardinal Ottaviani, had succeeded brilliantly.

Incredibly, no more than fifty ultra-conservative cardinals and bishops, compared to the 2,500 total delegates in attendance at Vatican Council II, had successfully prevented any meaningful accomplishments in the First Session and only one in the Second Session (conducting religious services in local languages instead of Latin).

Furthermore, the conservatives were well positioned to bring this Third Session to a similarly abortive end, with the objective of making it the very last meeting of the ill-fated Vatican Council II.

For the Opening Ceremony, Pope Paul was again carried into St. Peter's Basilica on the *sedia gestatoria*. However, he had a surprise in store. As soon as he reached the altar and dismounted, he was joined by twenty-four cardinals and bishops with whom he intended to concelebrate the Mass. This remarkable image was striking to all in attendance; heartening to most, alarming to a powerful few. And the symbolism was crystal clear. Pope Paul was signaling that the doctrine of Collegiality, calling for a greater "collegial" or advisory role for cardinals and bishops in conducting Church affairs alongside the pope, was going to be a priority for the Third Session.

Collegiality was a holdover from the Second Session that had been vehemently opposed by staunch traditionalists, who saw it as a dangerous affront to the absolute papal authority that had presided over the Roman Catholic Church for centuries. This papal supremacy was further affirmed during Vatican Council I in 1870, which also proclaimed the pope's infallibility when speaking *ex cathedra* (from the chair) on official matters of Church doctrine and morality.

In his opening address, Pope Paul declared to the assembled prelates that he was absolutely committed to fulfilling the legacy of Pope John XXIII of bringing the Church into the modern world, *starting* with the doctrine of Collegiality. In addition, he said, there were still other crucial issues that needed to be addressed during this Third Session and he pledged to ensure that all voices would be heard in the coming weeks. At this statement there was an audible rumbling from the assembly, as many of those in attendance sincerely doubted his resolve. When Paul finished his sermon, he returned to the altar, said a quiet prayer, then gave a final blessing. As he descended from the altar, he slowly made his way down the long nave to tempered applause.

Within an hour of the Opening Ceremony's conclusion, Ernesto Cardinal Ruffini, an arch-conservative senior member of the Curia, was summoned by Cardinal Ottaviani to a secret meeting in his office. Also called was Archbishop Pericle Felici, the Presiding Secretary General of the Council. Already present was Archbishop Pietro Parente, Ottaviani's second-in-command in the Holy Office. All four had been caught by surprise at Pope Paul's audacious declaration to pursue the doctrine of Collegiality, not to mention his shameless concelebration of the Mass to emphasize his intentions.

"Never in the 2,000-year history of the Church has a pope taken such a condemnable stroke to the Throne of St. Peter!" railed Cardinal Ottaviani to his colleagues. "Will last century's Vatican Council I now be thrown asunder as well?" In his mind, and certainly those of the others in the room, a dangerous crossroads was at hand. "The pope is pandering to progressives who only react to the winds of the present without deference to the past," growled Ottaviani. "And *they* are being encouraged by the articles of that damnable Xavier Rynne!" He rose to close his office door. "We must respond aggressively…and *now!*"

Conciliar business was to begin the following day, Tuesday, September 15, 1964, with a welcome by Archbishop Felici. That morning, however, instead of the traditional opening, the archbishop immediately launched into a steely warning: "*Anyone* discussing conciliar proceedings outside of the Council Hall will be breaking the Vatican Oath of Secrecy. They will face excommunication!" he thundered.

The delegates were taken aback by this startling beginning to the very first gathering of the Third Session. Murphy, in an overlooking balcony, was particularly alarmed. *Was that directed at me?* he asked himself.

Indeed, it most certainly was.

———◆———

The next morning there was a letter awaiting Pope Paul when he arrived at his office. It had been signed by fourteen prelates, including all of the cardinals in the Roman Curia and a handful of conservative Italian bishops. The letter "strongly urged" that he immediately remove the doctrine of Collegiality from the Council's agenda; in the minds of the letter's signers it was "replete with heresy." Paul scanned the list of signatories. Pointing to one name, halfway down the list, he said to his personal secretary, Father Pasquale Macchi, "*This* is the man responsible, and he has neither the courtesy nor the courage to acknowledge sole authorship." The signature was that of Alfredo Cardinal Ottaviani.

"And so it begins," Pope Paul remarked, disconsolate.

Later that day, Father Macchi appeared unannounced at the office of Cardinal Ottaviani, who bade him to enter. He took a deep breath. "The Holy Father would like to express his profound disappointment in the signatories of that letter," Macchi said, "and particularly in Your Eminence." He then simply turned and walked out.

Ottaviani was outraged, not only because the pope did not officially respond in writing to the letter but that he had sent a lowly personal secretary to deliver his curt verbal reply.

Following Macchi's departure, Ottaviani summoned Archbishop Parente. "I will *not* allow this doctrine of Collegiality, this Council, to undo thousands of years of papal preeminence!" he railed. He slowly composed himself, thought for a moment, then continued: "As Isaiah warned, 'Those who guide this people are leading them astray.'"

Parente remained silent, not sure where this was going.

"Unfortunately," the cardinal said pensively, "we may not be able to actually *prevent* the passage of this heretical document on Collegiality, but there may still be a way to *undermine* it." He thought for a moment then said, "Archbishop, I will need your help."

Parente smiled conspiratorially.

On the morning of September 21ˢᵗ, it was Archbishop
Parente's turn to deliver a shock to the Council Fathers
when he stood up, approached the microphone, and
surprisingly argued that the doctrine of Collegiality
should *not* be considered a threat to traditional papal
authority and should therefore be approved by the
Council. This was completely against everything that
the conservative minority had so aggressively espoused
during the Second Session, and the gathered delegates
were astonished.

"I am not speaking as an official of the Holy Office
but simply as a bishop," Parente offered. "The very word
collegium," he noted, "has evoked undue terror on the part
of some." He scanned the astounded faces throughout the
basilica. "However," he continued, slowly, for full effect,
"such fears are *groundless.*" He paused, appreciating the
stunned silence. "Let me be clear," he continued. "I firmly
believe that the doctrine of Collegiality should be open for
full debate by the Council."

Once the amazement at Parente's declaration subsided, a non-binding straw vote was immediately proposed
and seconded. The Council Fathers did not dare miss this
unexpected opportunity for what could very likely become
the centerpiece accomplishment of the Third Session. It
passed with near unanimity, with the notable support of
every single cardinal in the Curia.

After the vote was tallied, Father Murphy watched Parente quietly leave the basilica with a curious smile clearly evident on his face.

———◆———

"What the hell is happening?" Murphy asked his similarly bewildered dinner companions Benelli and Macchi once they were seated. At the request of Murphy, they were meeting at a new location, a café called Sebastiani's, though he did not explain the reason for the change from La Carbonara. Nonetheless, it happened to be much closer to Benelli's and Macchi's respective apartments and, importantly, as one passed through the outdoor café and descended the stairs from the busy Via Cola di Rienzo, it was an extremely private venue.

Murphy continued, "Ottaviani and his gang fought so hard against Collegiality in the Second Session. It simply doesn't make sense."

"Pope Paul was caught off guard as well," added Macchi. "And Parente's speech was on the heels of an astonishing letter that was delivered to His Holiness only a few days prior. It was signed by the leaders of the conservative coalition, pleading with the pope to *cancel* any discussion of Collegiality outright! And then Parente's speech..." Macchi shook his head. "His Holiness said to me, 'Maybe they are coming around,' although I doubt he half-believed it."

"There is something afoot," conjectured a skeptical Benelli. "Too much effort was put forth by the conservatives to quash Collegiality. And then to simply give up?"

"Well, it will become apparent soon enough," said Murphy, unaware how prescient his comment would be.

The debate on Collegiality continued unabated for weeks, with a record number of cardinals and bishops rising to get on the official record with their support for this historic document – all being encouraged by the solicitous Archbishop Felici. Importantly, Felici had waived the normal time limits for each speaker, thus extending the debate on this single schema much longer than had been originally scheduled. Almost without notice, at least by the overly enthusiastic Council Fathers, almost a third of the time allotted for the entire Third Session had quickly elapsed.

When he finally brought the debate to a close, Archbishop Felici announced that, because so many additional details would have to be incorporated into the final text, it would be forwarded to Cardinal Ottaviani's Theological Commission for further review and revision. This seemed innocuous enough to the delegates, given the surprising support for the doctrine from virtually every conservative prelate, including Ottaviani himself. Felici promised that a final draft would be ready for a full Council vote by the last week of the Third Session.

With widespread anticipation of its first major accomplishment seemingly a *fait accompli,* the Council Fathers optimistically turned to debating the next schema on its agenda, the all-important Declaration on Religious Liberty and the Jews, which proclaimed: the importance of freedom of religion for all; equality among all Christian religions; and a denunciation of the historic blame directed against the Jews for the death of Jesus Christ.

There was very little controversy with the call for universal freedom of religion. And the overwhelming majority of the Council Fathers demanded that Vatican Council II reject once and for all the contention that the Jewish people should ever be accused of *deicide* (literally "the killing of God") in the death of Jesus Christ.

However, the conservative minority was surprisingly aggressive in its condemnation of the second part of the schema regarding equality among religions. Over the centuries, the classic Roman Catholic position was self-proclaimed preeminence over all other Christian denominations as well as Judaism and other faiths. "The Declaration should be entitled 'On Religious Tolerance,' not 'Liberty,'" shouted Cardinal Ruffini from the microphone during an impassioned speech. "Those in error have no rights!" he yelled, clearly referencing the other religions.

Gasps at Ruffini's outrageous comment were heard throughout the basilica. What had been originally foreseen as a straightforward debate with minimal dissension now looked like it would be mired in protracted acrimony. As such, Archbishop Felici announced an immediate cessation to the debate, declaring that he would instead create a brand new committee to facilitate its further review. Not only was the unilateral creation of a new committee in clear violation of the established Council rules but it further angered the delegates when they were told that this committee would be co-chaired by Cardinal Ottaviani.

In response to this obvious attempt to stall the Declaration on Religious Liberty and the Jews, a group of twelve incensed non-Curial cardinals met at the residence of Josef Cardinal Frings of Germany. They drafted a petition to Pope Paul deploring the sudden creation of that new committee which, they all knew, was a disingenuous tactic to destroy any chance of the Declaration's passage. Starting with the powerful phrase *"Magno cum dolore* – With great pain,"* the letter was transcribed as follows:

Holy Father,

[*Magno cum dolore*] With great pain we have learned that the Declaration on Religious Liberty and the Jews, although in accord with the desire of the great majority of the Fathers, is to be entrusted to a newly created committee, members of whom appear to be opposed to the orientation of the majority of the Council in this matter.

This news is for us a source of extreme anxiety and very disquieting. Countless men throughout the world know that this Declaration has already been prepared, and they also know the sense in which it has been drafted. In such an important matter, any appearance of a violation of the rules of the Council, and its freedom, would be extremely prejudicial to the whole Church in the light of world opinion.

Impelled by this anxiety, we ask Your Holiness with great insistence that the Declaration be returned to the normal procedure of the Council and dealt with according to the existing rules, so that there may not result from it great evils for the whole People of God.

The letter was hand-delivered to Pope Paul by Cardinal Frings. Upon reading it, the pope acknowledged that he, too, was deeply disturbed by Archbishop Felici's unsanctioned, unilateral bypassing of existing Council protocol. He assured Frings that the Declaration on Religious Liberty and the Jews in its current form would remain open for debate. The German cardinal left somewhat mollified but still unsure of the pope's resolve to act against the powerful Curia on this matter. In fact, Frings' misgivings were well founded. In defiance of the pope's intentions, the schema on Religious Liberty and the Jews would languish in "committee review" without further debate for the entirety of the Third Session.

At this point, concern arose whether it would be realistically possible to bring Vatican Council II to a close at the end of the Third Session or whether a Fourth Session would be required to address the many critical issues currently facing the Church. A majority of the attendees were in clear support of a Fourth Session. However, as expected, the conservative minority was adamantly opposed. Pope Paul would have to decide.

On Tuesday, October 20, 1964, with just over four weeks to go in the Third Session, the Council Fathers were presented with the long-awaited schema on The Church in the Modern World. This would frame the Council's debates on an incredibly wide range of contemporary societal issues: the use of birth control by married couples; combating racism and discrimination; encouraging international economic support for the poorest countries; and even discussing the morality of war and use of the atomic bomb among other pressing topics.

First to be addressed was the Church's stance on the use of birth control, specifically within the marriage covenant. Cardinal Ottaviani wasted no time interjecting his strong opinion: "I am not pleased with the statement of the text that married couples can determine the number of children they are to have. This has never been sanctioned in the Church!" he bellowed. "Are we to ignore God's commandment in Genesis, 'Be fruitful and multiply?'" He continued in a more personal vein. "This priest who speaks to you now is the eleventh of twelve children, whose father was a laborer in a bakery. I purposely say laborer, not the owner of a bakery. My parents never doubted Providence. I issue a warning to you bishops: Can the Church possibly have erred for so many centuries?"

He stomped off the podium and took his seat, overcome with emotion. However, speaker after speaker then approached the microphone with contrarian arguments that it was necessary to loosen the controlling grasp of the Church within the marriage relationship. Cardinal Ottaviani could not fathom such outrageous heresy so he stormed out of the basilica. Archbishop Felici, in deference to his colleague, immediately closed debate on the issue, ironically to the relief of many in attendance who were worried that this single issue would otherwise consume the bulk of the remaining weeks in the Third Session. Similarly, over the next two weeks, other topics within the schema on The Church in the Modern World resulted in combative, inconclusive, and eventually premature dismissals.

As the Council entered its next to last week on November 9th, the initial atmosphere of cautious optimism had changed perceptibly to one of mounting gloom. The major worry was over the fate of the doctrine of Collegiality, which had received near unanimous approval in the straw vote weeks earlier but was still "under review" by the Theological Commission. Only with direct pressure from

Pope Paul himself was the document grudgingly released by the commission for a final vote. Alarmingly, though, it now contained a new, extremely detailed, multi-page "Explanatory Note" that had not been included in the original text. This note significantly minimized, in subtle but very important ways, the collegial role that cardinals and bishops would play in advising the pope. Because of the impact of the new wording, another round of debate would have normally been warranted. However, with the Third Session rapidly coming to a close, the majority of Council Fathers decided that rather than risk having no doctrine at all, it was better to approve an imperfect document. In the end, the neutralized doctrine of Collegiality passed by an overwhelming but disgruntled majority. The conservative faction, led by Cardinal Ottaviani, could claim at least a partial victory.

———

The following week, when the text on Religious Liberty and the Jews was again scheduled for debate, Eugène Cardinal Tisserant, a Curial confidante of Cardinal Ottaviani, suddenly rose and put an immediate stop to the discussion with the following pronouncement:

> Several Fathers are of the opinion that not enough time has been allowed for an appropriate examination of the text on Religious Liberty and the Jews, which appears to be an essentially new document. Therefore,

it has been deemed best by the Council presidents, in conformity with the rules, not to proceed to a vote during this session as previously announced.

Tisserant's shocking announcement was met with catcalls and protests throughout the assembly. The delegates felt cheated, betrayed, insulted, and humiliated. Pandemonium broke out on the Council floor.

Amidst the chaos, Albert Cardinal Meyer of Chicago, normally a calm and dignified figure, got up from his seat to directly confront Cardinal Tisserant. However, before he could utter a word, he was met with Tisserant's raised hand and emphatic dismissal, "The decision has been made, and it is *final!*"

Meyer, incensed, stalked away and joined a group of furious prelates gathered on the left side of the nave. Bishop Francis Reh of New York shouted, "Let's not stand here talking! Who's got some paper?" With the help of several other bishops, a petition to Pope Paul was hastily written out by hand and copied on multiple sheets:

Your Holiness,

With reverence but urgently, very urgently, most urgently, we request that a vote on the Declaration on Religious Liberty and the Jews be taken before the end of this session of the Council, lest the confidence of the world, both Christian and non-Christian, be lost.

Copies were circulated and signatures collected as dozens of clerics moved up and down the banked tiers of seats. When the canvassing was completed, more than 1,000 signatures had been collected, no small feat considering the limited time in which it had to be done.

Cardinal Meyer, along with Joseph Cardinal Ritter of St. Louis and Paul-Emile Cardinal Léger of Montreal, then left the basilica to hand-carry their entreaty to the pope. When Pope Paul read the petition, he rebuffed them, making the excuse that he preferred not to interfere in the Council's actions. However, seeing the extreme anger on their faces, he promised that the Declaration on Religious Liberty and the Jews would be the first order of business in the upcoming Fourth Session. The cardinals were not even remotely satisfied, having already lost trust in this pope's ability to counter the scheming endeavors of the powerful conservative coalition.

The next morning, Archbishop Felici again gave the floor to Cardinal Tisserant, who rose and read in a stern monotone the following:

Many Fathers were deeply disappointed by the announcement yesterday that the vote on Religious Liberty and the Jews was to be postponed and they petitioned the Holy Father that a vote be taken before the end of this session. In the name of the Supreme Pontiff, I wish to make the following announcement: The request that voting be delayed was granted because, according to the Rules of the

Council, it had to be granted out of respect for the freedom of the Fathers in their desire to examine fully and in accordance with the rules for a document of such great importance. That is why the schema for the Declaration on Religious Liberty and the Jews will be treated in the next session and, if possible, before any other matters.

There was stunned silence throughout the basilica. Hundreds of cardinals and bishops stood up and walked out in protest.

———◆———

Along with the dual subterfuge of the last-minute addition of the Explanatory Note in the doctrine of Collegiality and of the postponement of a vote on Religious Liberty and the Jews, the Council received a third thunderbolt involving the next item on its agenda, the Decree on Oriental Churches, which was to establish an initial dialogue toward reconciliation between the Roman Catholic and Christian Orthodox religions. This document was especially dear to Pope Paul after his meeting with Patriarch Athenagoras in Jerusalem. However, it faced a strong backlash from conservatives in the Curia, who contended that it would put the Catholic and Orthodox churches on an equal footing. Interestingly, and not coincidentally, according to many of the Council Fathers, Archbishop Felici suddenly announced that the debate on this schema would have to be postponed indefinitely because "physical printing" of the final schema "was taking longer than expected." It would therefore not be available until the very last days of the session. The Council Fathers would not have a chance to adequately review the Decree on Oriental Churches before casting their final ballots.

⸻

By the end of the Third Session, only three documents would be voted on and approved by the Council: the newly-christened "Constitution on the Church" (which contained the doctrine of Collegiality) that gave at least some influence (albeit far more limited than desired) to cardinals and bishops in formulating Church policy alongside the pope; the Decree on Oriental Churches, to begin the process of reconciliation with Orthodox Christian denominations; and a last-minute Decree on Ecumenism that encouraged communication among all Christian communities. The latter two were presented to the Council Fathers with virtually no time for review. More than a dozen other schema, most notably those concerning The Church in the Modern World and Religious Liberty and the Jews were never even brought to the Council floor.

⸻

On Saturday morning, November 21, 1964, Pope Paul was carried into St. Peter's Basilica on the *sedia gestatoria* for the Closing Ceremony. As he passed by the tiers of stony-faced, silent cardinals in red caps and bishops in white mitres and copes, there was no applause. The strained feelings between Pope Paul and the assembled clerics was palpable.

After a solemn Mass, concelebrated with twenty of his brethren, the pope ascended the pulpit for his message to officially close the Third Session. He had expected that there would at least be a positive response when he announced the successful passage of the Constitution on the Church (Collegiality) and the Decrees on the Oriental Churches and Ecumenism, all three milestones on the road to *aggiornamento*, but the applause was tepid at best.

The pope told the assembly that there was still significant work yet required of the Council Fathers and that a Fourth but final Session of Vatican Council II would be necessary. Given the widespread disappointment over the preceding ten weeks, his pronouncement was not unexpected.

After blessing the congregation, the grim-faced pope walked slowly down the central aisle amid weighty silence and quietly left the basilica. The contrast with the closing of the First Session under Pope John could not have been more striking.

Immediately after the Closing Ceremony, Father Murphy hurried to his apartment at the Accademia Alfonsiana and began typing in an emotional rage his column for *The New Yorker:*

The steady succession of subversive maneuvers by the small, yet powerful conservative minority of Curial and Italian prelates, led by Alfredo Cardinal Ottaviani, was outrageous....

Pandemonium broke out on the Council floor. No one had ever seen such a spectacle in the sacred basilica of St. Peter's....

From one American prelate's lips, the deeply felt words "The bastards!" burst forth. He was speaking for all of his shocked and disbelieving colleagues....

One would have to go back to an early Church Council – that of Trent, say, when an enraged bishop pulled another's beard – to find a precedent for the scene of consternation, outrage, and disarray that took place here during the last week of the Third Session of Vatican II....[7]

Pope Paul was exhausted, depressed, and alone in his papal office after returning from the Closing Ceremony. He noticed that his window had been left open and droplets from an intermittent rain were sprinkling onto the sill. He went over to close it but hesitated, then knelt, taking pleasure in the cooling mist on his face. He prayed for guidance and strength. He reflected on the Gospel of Matthew where Jesus said to his disciples, "If anyone wishes to

[7] "Letter from Vatican City," *The New Yorker*, January 9, 1965

come after Me, he must take up his cross and follow Me."
The legacy of Pope John's *aggiornamento*, the success or
failure of Vatican Council II, was Pope Paul's cross to bear.
And it was proving too much.

The next morning he met with Monsignor Benelli and
Father Macchi. To their relief he seemed mercifully well
rested and surprisingly energized. In the middle of their
review of his scheduled meetings with departing cardinals
and bishops, Paul interjected and said, "I would like to
attend the upcoming Eucharistic Congress in Bombay."

Neither Benelli nor Macchi was surprised at the
pope's decision; he had taken a similar international trip
to Jerusalem after the discouraging end to the Second Session. It was a way for him to step away from disappointment, to shift the narrative of his papacy to something
positive, something more in his control. This Eucharistic
Congress would also be especially poignant as it would
mark the first time that a Roman Pontiff would visit
India, providing strong support for the Catholic minority
in that country.

With impressive logistical effort, Benelli and Macchi
quickly put together a schedule for the pope's trip. Less
than two weeks later he flew from Rome and landed in
Bombay to a wildly enthusiastic reception. Over the next
three days he met with local religious leaders and youth
groups, celebrated more than a dozen Masses in front of
huge audiences, and blessed immense crowds of all faiths
that lined the streets as he passed. He even composed a
special prayer, quoted from the Upanishads, that he shared

at each stop. The Indian people began calling him *bada guru,* "great holy man."

By all accounts, the pope's trip to India was a resounding success. Oddly enough, it was a pro-Communist weekly, *Blitz,* that carried the most memorable description of his visit: "We have seen Eisenhower, Khrushchev, Chou, the Shah of Persia, the Queen of England, Nasser, Tito, Sukarno, and others ride in glory through our capital during the mighty Nehru epoch, but this humble pilgrim of God and Vicar of Christ got a reception that surpassed them all."

Upon his return to Rome, Pope Paul was reinvigorated. "I now have the strength to bear my cross," he told Benelli and Macchi. "We have much to do. Let us begin."

———

Shortly after the close of the Third Session, Murphy received an invitation from Luciana to meet for cocktails and dinner at Harry's Bar, the upscale lounge adjacent to the Villa Borghese gardens. In spite of its American name, Harry's had been founded by an Italian restauranteur, Arrigo Cipriani, and had an international reputation for both its signature cocktails and exceptional regional Italian cuisine.

As Murphy entered, there was an immediate feeling of timeless elegance, the perfect venue for Luciana, he thought. He was met by a hostess who was expecting his arrival and escorted him to a table in a rear corner. There awaited Luciana and, surprisingly, an older male friend. He was well dressed in a suit and tie, with a fedora in his lap.

"I have missed you terribly, Frank," Luciana said as she extended her hand. "And please may I introduce Signor Giovanni Ricci," she said. "He was a lifelong friend of Cardinal Tardini, God rest his soul, and has remained a loyal supporter of the children at the Villa Nazareth orphanage."

Signor Ricci nodded in greeting, although he did not stand to shake Murphy's hand. He was somewhat overweight, with fleshy jowls and circles under his eyes, but he exuded a definite aura of self-importance. He did not smile; it did not seem to come naturally to him.

"Let us catch up," Luciana offered, and an exceptional meal with light conversation, mostly between Luciana and Murphy, ensued.

After dessert, Luciana excused herself and an uncomfortable silence followed. Eventually Signor Ricci spoke up. "I can be a very good friend to you," he said in a gravelly whisper. "A very generous friend."

Murphy, surprised and somewhat bewildered at the remark, did not respond. The silence continued.

Luciana finally returned and looked at the two of them, smiling at their discomfort. As soon as she was seated, she said, "If I may, Frank, I know that you have been very busy with Vatican affairs, but I hope that you have not forgotten the children of Villa Nazareth."

"No, indeed I have not," Murphy replied. "This past summer I corresponded with a number of American families who I had helped while in Germany and received some positive notes in return. I expect more will be forthcoming."

"Wonderful. Simply wonderful," Luciana said with obvious relief, glancing at Signor Ricci. "There are already profiles for most of the children at the orphanage." She then added, "As to overcoming some challenges with…"

She was quickly interrupted by Signor Ricci. "If I may," he apologized, then turned to Murphy, "we have good friends in the Ministry of Foreign Affairs, who can give ready permission for the expatriation of adopted children to America, and also in the Police Headquarters, who can issue their passports. We are in a position to make the adoption process much easier," he said, "…as well as to show friends our gratitude."

Murphy grimaced. It was obvious to him what Signor Ricci was insinuating.

Luciana saw the concern on Murphy's face. "Frank, we only ask you to help us locate families in America for these children. We will take care of the rest," she said, hoping to ease his angst.

The meal ended uncomfortably, and Murphy took his leave, politely kissing Luciana on the cheek and reaching to shake the still-seated Signor Ricci's hand.

"I do not know," Ricci said as he watched Murphy walk away. "I am not so sure."

"But I am," said Luciana, albeit somewhat unconvincingly.

"That bastard!" yelled Cardinal Ottaviani to no one in particular as he sat fuming in his Vatican office. He held in his hands the most recent issue of *The New Yorker* that detailed the failures of the Third Session of the Council and put the blame squarely on him and his Curial colleagues. "He was warned!" he screeched. "HE WAS WARNED!!!"

On the night of January 30th, Murphy had a message hand-delivered to him at his apartment in the Accademia Alfonsiana by Archbishop Parente's personal secretary, Father Antonio Bianchi, requiring him to appear at the Holy Office the following morning at 10:00. It stated that he would be interrogated under the Vatican Oath of Secrecy, with the penalty of excommunication if he refused. When Murphy inquired as to the subject matter for the oath, Bianchi explained that he would be informed only upon his arrival at the Holy Office.

The next morning Murphy sought out both Francis Cardinal Spellman of New York and John Cardinal Heenan of Westminster, England, and explained to them that he was being summoned to the Holy Office. When they inquired as to the nature of the summons, he gave a vague response about possibly overstepping his role as a Council *peritus*, purposefully not mentioning his pseudonymous authorship of *The New Yorker* articles. They could not hide their alarm, understanding full well the potential consequences of this extremely rare tribunal. Spellman led the three of them in a quick but fervent prayer, then Murphy hurried off.

He arrived a few minutes early to the Holy Office and waited anxiously for Archbishop Parente, who entered promptly at the appointed hour. He was accompanied by two priests, one of whom was Father Bianchi and the other Father Henry Cosgrove, an acquaintance of Murphy's from Brooklyn.

"Kneel down," commanded Archbishop Parente, "and you will take the Oath of Secrecy."

"Not until I know why," Murphy responded nervously.

"I will tell you after the oath."

"No," Murphy replied more firmly. "I am not taking an oath about something for which I do not know the substance."

"You will be told..."

"No, archbishop," Murphy interrupted. "And what are these two gentlemen doing here?"

"One is my secretary, the other a translator."

"I do not need a translator," Murphy responded. "Henry," he said, turning to the American cleric, "you can be my secretary." Cosgrove nervously nodded his assent.

Murphy asked if Parente wanted to interrogate him regarding the copy of *The New Yorker* with little pieces of paper that he had tucked under his arm. "Yes," Parente confirmed, his temper rising. Murphy then agreed to take the Oath of Secrecy but clarified that his responses would be specifically limited to what he might know regarding that particular magazine. He then knelt, affirmed the oath, and rose.

Parente began reading a series of excerpts from *The New Yorker*. For each Murphy agreed that they were written by one Xavier Rynne, but carefully added that he was Father Francis Murphy. Parente became increasingly frustrated at Murphy's clever use of casuistry. Then Parente came to a defamatory passage written about himself, describing his expulsion from Rome some twenty years earlier by Pope Pius XI.

"Listen," Parente said after reading it aloud, "you understand that Pius XI was a little sick in the head."

Shocked at Parente's outrageous attack on a Roman Pontiff, Murphy shouted to his newly-acquired secretary, "Henry, write that down!"

Parente immediately realized the significance of what he had just said, a possibly blasphemous offense in the strictest interpretation of the Holy Office. Flustered, he ceased the interrogation and stormed out of the room. Murphy, Bianchi, and Cosgrove stood there motionless, stunned, uncertain what to do. Finally, Murphy whispered an impromptu closing prayer, dismissed both priests, then walked rapidly back to his apartment.

"They are certainly not done," he grumbled nervously to himself. "But neither am I." With renewed resolve, he began writing his next article for *The New Yorker*, his most passionate yet:

The atmosphere of optimism surrounding Vatican Council II, whose Fourth Session opens on September 14th, has been tempered by a feeling of uncertainty owing to Pope Paul's rather equivocal attitude of late....

One disturbing consequence of the pope's failure to act is the widespread impression that he is being controlled by the conservative minority around him, which is opposed to the Council, or that, at the very least, he underestimates the danger from this quarter....

In a statement this summer, the head of the Holy Office, Cardinal Ottaviani, declared himself in flat opposition to the papal policy of carrying on any dialogue with Communists and atheists. Clearly, the Curial prelate has no conception of Christianity as a positive value. In effect, this attitude amounts to saying that modern man can literally go to Hell unless he is willing to accept the Christian message on his, Cardinal Ottaviani's, terms....

Historically, the Curia has always attempted to control the Church in a dictatorial fashion....

Thus far, the pope has displayed an extreme reluctance to intervene openly in the Council's deliberations and, on the few occasions when he has found it necessary to assert his authority, he has caused near fiascos....

The world is now asking whether Pope Paul will have the courage to emulate his mentor, Pius XII, who once said with respect to liturgical renewal, "I will move so far with the reform that a return will be made impossible." If Paul does, the important thing for him and the Church is to keep the doors open. After all, Christ Himself, as we are told in the third chapter of the Book of Revelations, laid down as an eternal law: "Behold, I have caused doors to be opened before thee, which no one can shut."[8]

————◆————

Pope Paul was bitterly discouraged by the overwhelmingly negative coverage in the press about the failures of the Third Session. As he complained to Monsignor Benelli, "I read in the newspapers that I am timid, that I cannot make up my mind and am torn by conflicting advice." Almost in a whisper he added, "I may perhaps be slow. But I know what I want." Then, raising his voice and with surprising conviction he said, "It is now time to act."

As a first step, he crafted a long-overdue letter to all of the cardinals in the Curia: "From now on you will show complete docility – unquestioned obedience and compliance – to the reforms which will be decreed in the upcoming Fourth Session." He added in no uncertain terms, "You will further refrain from any controversial comments that, quite frankly, do more harm than good to the Curia itself." This was a clear allusion to a remark made by an "anonymous" Curial cardinal in the Italian press who characterized the delegates to Vatican Council II as "thousands of good-for-nothings, many of whom, in spite of the pectoral

---

[8] "Letter from Vatican City," *The New Yorker*, September 11, 1965

crosses around their necks, don't believe in the true teachings of the Catholic Church."

As his next act, Pope Paul ordered the immediate release of a comprehensive biography of Galileo written some thirty years earlier by the late Monsignor Pio Paschini, a renowned Roman Catholic historian. The original manuscript had been impounded by the Holy Office on spurious grounds regarding Paschini's academic credentials. The real reason, however, was the Holy Office's continuing reluctance to acknowledge any historic transgression by the Catholic Church in the case of Galileo, who was threatened with excommunication for his supposedly heretical proposition that the earth revolves around the sun.

To underscore this action, Pope Paul traveled to Pisa, the site of Galileo's famous experiments, to emphasize the rehabilitation of the astronomer in the eyes of the Church more than three hundred years after his forced recantation and humiliation by the Holy Inquisition in 1633. Paul encouraged the crowd of over 100,000 gathered in front of the 11th-century marble baptistry of the cathedral to "imitate the faith of Galileo in the wholesale pursuit of truth," and he asked for their prayers in this regard for the upcoming Fourth Session of Vatican Council II.

Next, Pope Paul announced a plan to establish a brand new Synod of Bishops, to be 150 clerics strong, as a direct affront to the entrenched power base of the cardinals in the Curia. This would also be a powerful affirmation of the doctrine of Collegiality, promulgated during the Third

Session, that called for the increased involvement of cardinals and bishops in advising the pope on Church affairs.

Finally, in his general audience on July 28th, Pope Paul announced an incredibly ambitious agenda for the Fourth Session. "The number and nature of the themes to be dealt with, their gravity and complexity, as well as the fact that this upcoming session will mark the end of Vatican Council II, all pose an extraordinary challenge for the Church … and it will be met."

A similar conviction for action was rapidly spreading among the non-Curial Council Fathers, who had been roundly chastised upon their returns home after the ineffectual first three sessions of Vatican Council II. In no small measure, they had also become significantly emboldened by the now widely disseminated articles of Xavier Rynne, who had single-handedly exposed the pernicious efforts of Cardinal Ottaviani and the powerful Curial coalition to undermine the proceedings of Vatican Council II.

The stage was now set for a final, historic confrontation.

CHAPTER X

———◆———

"*Ite in pace* –
Go in peace."

From the moment Pope Paul entered St. Peter's Basilica on September 14, 1965, to convene the Fourth Session of Vatican Council II, it became apparent to the assembled 2,500 cardinals and bishops that he intended to take a much firmer hand in the proceedings – and to do so in his own personal fashion. Gone was the pageantry that usually preceded papal processions. He walked down the central nave on foot rather than being carried upon the *sedia gestatoria,* and he was accompanied only by the twenty-six bishops who would be concelebrating the solemn opening Mass with him.

Paul was vested in a simple cope instead of the elaborate and unwieldy papal mantle and was no longer wearing the papal tiara but only a mitre similar to those of his fellow bishops. He carried a pastoral staff in the form of a cross which he was later said to have designed himself.

Paul's opening address neither touched on any of the issues that had plagued the Third Session nor did he outline the many pressing matters still pending before the Council. Rather, he took the occasion to reaffirm his broader goals beyond the Council's direct purview, most notably his intention to put in place his promised Synod of Bishops, thus signaling his determination to implement the Third Session's doctrine of Collegiality that called for an increased role for cardinals and bishops in assisting the pope with Church affairs.

This pronouncement was met with immediate, widespread applause, with the conspicuous exception of the cardinals of the Curia seated in the rows nearest the altar. The pope followed with a surprise announcement that he planned to attend the upcoming United Nations General Assembly in early October. There he would make a personal appeal for worldwide peace, especially timely given the escalating war in Southeast Asia. He then closed with a prayer of hope that the forthcoming Council proceedings would be "orderly and profitable" and that the "hearts of the assembled cardinals and bishops would remain open to the delicate, powerful, secret, and irresistible influence of the Spirit of Truth."

As he descended from the altar and made his way back down the nave, a feeling of cautious optimism seemed to envelope the congregation.

He may actually succeed, thought Frank Murphy while he watched from the balcony as Pope Paul exited the basilica.

Murphy was expecting Giovanni Benelli and Pasquale Macchi to meet him immediately after the Opening Ceremony. He had walked to Sebastiani's to reserve a private table for them toward the back of the restaurant. After waiting impatiently for close to an hour, he decided to go ahead and order lunch, eating impassively as they still had not appeared. Finally, just as he finished, both priests arrived, exhausted but exhilarated.

Murphy stood up and warmly embraced his two friends; he had seen little of them over the course of the summer and not at all in the weeks leading up to the opening of the Fourth Session.

"Well," Murphy began, "it looks like we have a new and improved Pope Paul, eh?"

Benelli and Macchi looked at each other and smiled in agreement. "Yes indeed," Benelli said. "And apologies for being late. We have just left the most extraordinary meeting." He paused while the waiter approached to take their drink orders; both simply asked for water.

"The past few months have been extremely busy, Benelli began. "The Holy Father has been personally involved in the work of every commission that has been preparing schema for the Fourth Session, most notably the Theological Commission, to the clear displeasure of Cardinal Ottaviani." Both Benelli and Macchi laughed at this. "He is determined not to fail; quite frankly, he must not. He must succeed."

The waiter returned with the water, saw that they were not yet ready to order, and stepped away.

"He has also met with many groups of cardinals and bishops upon their arrival in Rome," added Benelli. "He has given each of them his solemn vow that this session will be different."

"We will see," said a skeptical Murphy.

"To that point," interjected Macchi, "you must realize that the articles appearing in *The New Yorker* from Xavier Rynne have had a powerful influence on the delegates. We heard this first-hand from many of them, as did the Holy Father. They are universally emboldened, thanks in great measure to you," Macchi said with clear pride. "I mean, to Xavier Rynne," he added with a chuckle.

"But their knowledge of the authorship?" asked Murphy nervously.

"As far as we know, they are not aware," said Benelli.

"But the Ottaviani forces are still at work," Murphy added glumly.

Benelli looked at Macchi and they both nodded, which caught Murphy's attention.

"What?" Murphy asked.

There was a pause, then Benelli began again. "Immediately after the Opening Ceremony today, the pope summoned Cardinal Ottaviani to his private office in the papal residence. We were also present; that is the reason we are late."

"Why?" Murphy asked.

"The pontiff reminded the cardinal of his recent trip to Pisa in which he exhorted the crowd to 'imitate the faith of Galileo in the wholesale pursuit of truth,'" said Benelli.

"And Ottaviani visibly cringed at the mention of Galileo, as was the pontiff's intent," Macchi added with a devious smirk.

"The Holy Father then pulled out his personal Bible," Benelli continued, "marked with a passage from the Gospel of John, and read: 'And you will know the truth, and the truth will set you free.' He looked directly at Cardinal Ottaviani and smiled ruefully, 'I know the truth about you, Eminence, and it has indeed set me free.'"

"I'll be damned," said Murphy. "I'll…be…*damned.*"

***

The next morning as the Council Fathers were settling in for the first business meeting of the Fourth Session, Archbishop Pericle Felici, the Presiding Secretary General of the Council, approached the microphone and announced the unexpected arrival of Pope Paul. The pope quietly entered the basilica through a side door, accompanied only by his two aides, Monsignor Benelli and Father Macchi. After assisting at the daily Mass, he took a seat that had been left open for him at the debate moderator's table. Then, before the day's proceedings began, he rose to declare that his promised Synod of Bishops would be instituted *immediately*. With that, the pope handed Archbishop

Felici a papal decree entitled *Apostolica Sollicitudo*, establishing the Synod as official papal advisers on a permanent basis. Of particular significance, he noted, was the provision that the majority of the Synod's membership was to be elected by national or regional conferences of bishops, with no involvement by the Roman Curia.

Amid resounding applause, the pope left the basilica through the same side door in which he had arrived. Symbolically, he asked that his chair at the moderator's table remain in place for the duration of the Council, signaling his commitment to ongoing papal oversight of the Council's proceedings.

The first item of business on the Council's agenda was to discuss the most important holdover from the Third Session, the Declaration on Religious Liberty and the Jews. The first chapter of that schema, on Religious Liberty, declared that every individual has an inherent right to freedom of religious expression; it was to be the initial topic for debate. At Pope Paul's request, the second chapter concerning the Church's relationship with the Jews would be discussed separately to ensure that each topic could be fully addressed by the Council Fathers.

Richard Cardinal Cushing of Boston began the debate on Religious Liberty with an emphatic endorsement: "The promulgation of such a doctrine is a pastoral necessity of the first order for the whole world," he said, adding that there were many dictatorial governments that severely restricted human liberty, especially in religious matters. "Where citizens are denied the right to religious liberty, they are very often denied other civil liberties as well," Cushing emphasized.

Widespread approval followed his speech, with more than two dozen speakers rising to go on record with their support. It seemed likely that this first major schema of the Fourth Session would be quickly ratified; that is, until a series of conservative speakers unexpectedly rose to warn about its potential impact on fragile church/state relationships in certain countries and the risk of civil unrest and government crackdowns. Cardinal Ottaviani approached the microphone and added his voice to those in dissent. "Such a broad statement on Religious Liberty could do more harm than good, possibly even leading to the ultimate triumph of Communism!" he proclaimed.

Ottaviani's melodramatic foreboding was met with howls of derision, and even some irreverent laughter, but he was nonetheless followed by a half-dozen of his Curial colleagues nitpicking on specific wording in the schema, requesting additional clarifications, suggesting deletions of certain passages, etc. These obviously scripted efforts by the conservative faction were now widely recognized by the assembled delegates for what they were – a thinly veiled strategy to stall and eventually kill the schema.

Incredibly, the debate was suddenly brought to a close when Archbishop Felici came to the microphone to announce that all discussion on Religious Liberty would

be immediately halted so that a straw vote could be undertaken. Despite vehement protests by conservative prelates,
word quickly passed that the vote had been specifically
mandated by Pope Paul himself in a dramatic intervention.

Ballots were quickly distributed to the assembled delegates and tallied. The outcome was a staggering 1,997 in
favor of the Declaration on Religious Liberty in its present
form versus 224 opposed. Exuberant applause greeted the
result. Pope Paul had again signaled his determination to
make this Fourth Session successful and that he would
intervene whenever it was necessary.

The delegates were beginning to feel that the shadow
of the pope's previous acquiescence to the conservatives
during the Second and Third Sessions had suddenly been
lifted. It seemed possible that the Council might actually
finish its work by December – with tangible results to
show for its efforts.

The next day, debate was taken up on The Church in
the Modern World under the working title "Schema 13."
During the Third Session, the full schema was subjected
to scathing criticism by the conservative minority who
warned of the dangers of the Church interjecting itself into
the contemporary issues of society.

Schema 13 was the first ever document addressed "to
all mankind." It covered an incredibly wide range of topics, including: respect for human dignity; the nature of

marriage; the use of birth control; economic aid and development; capitalism versus communism; and the necessity of banishing all types of discrimination with regard to sex, race, and religion. It also stressed the importance of scientific research, admitting that the Church had sometimes erred in its attitude toward science in the past. It concluded with a call for peace and the avoidance of war throughout the world.

Over the next three weeks, heated debates unfolded as discussions on Schema 13 bounced haphazardly from one topic to the next with passionate, often diametrically opposed, viewpoints being aired. It was therefore decided to cease debate on the entire schema and send its various sub-parts to different conciliar commissions for further review, with the ambitious goal of having an all-inclusive consensus document ready for final debate before the end of the Fourth Session.

***

There was some powerful opposition to the pope's trip to the United Nations, led by the Curial elite. It was not so much the old-fashioned view of "It is enough for the Church to speak from Rome and wait for men to come to it," but rather their concern that Pope Paul's speech could have unforeseen implications for the Church. When they asked to review the text of his speech beforehand, Paul adamantly refused, thus further fueling their consternation.

The pope took a direct part in the planning of the trip: politely refusing a request by President Lyndon Johnson to meet him at the airport; insisting on taking the long route from Kennedy Airport through poverty-stricken Harlem, considered dangerous both by his entourage and the New York City police; and meeting beforehand with Protestant, Orthodox and Jewish representatives to the UN to underscore the fervency of the Council's objectives toward reconciliation with those religions.

Pope Paul's speech to the General Assembly marked the first time that a pope had addressed that body. He emphasized the need to do everything humanly possible to end the scourge of war and to promote disarmament. He also reiterated the Catholic Church's commitment to recognizing and protecting the inherent rights and freedoms of all individuals, regardless of nationality, race, or creed. He ended with an impassioned call for global cooperation to address issues of poverty, inequality, and underdevelopment.

The pope's speech was met with a standing ovation from the United Nations Assembly. According to the journalist Walter Lippman, "The pope said that the pursuit of peace transcends all other duties, and that the paramount crusade of mankind is the crusade against war and for peace," concluding that "...the Church has finally brought itself into the mainstream of human affairs."

The Vatican newspaper *L'Osservatore Romano* noted, "The trip appeared to most people as profoundly connected with the reforms of the Church now being carried out. The *aggiornamento* currently being undertaken has aroused a great hope in the hearts of mankind. They are convinced that what has begun will not go unfinished."

The Council Fathers were anxiously awaiting the pope's return from New York on Tuesday, October 5th, when word reached the Council floor that his TWA Boeing 707 had touched down at Rome's Fiumicino Airport at noon. Forty-five minutes later, the great bells of St. Peter's tolled as his black Mercedes rolled up to the steps in front of the main door of the basilica. Smiling and jubilant, as if it were the most casual thing in the world for a pope to travel halfway around the globe and back in thirty hours, he alighted from the car. Then, with unexpected energy, he quickly mounted the red-carpeted steps and walked briskly up the center aisle, with most of the cardinals and bishops applauding vigorously from their tiered seats. He then took his reserved place at the moderator's table. Aware that the morning's session had already been prolonged in order to receive him, he rose to give a brief, remarkably humble overview of his United Nations trip, after which he left the basilica by a side door amid the delegates' enthusiastic acclamation.

With clearly appropriate timing, the Council now began to discuss what some considered to be the most crucial chapter of Schema 13, the section on Peace and the Avoidance of War, which was the first to emerge from commission review. It delved into pressing matters regarding the horrors of modern warfare, the use of conventional versus atomic weapons, war crimes, just versus unjust wars, the "balance of terror," the right to conscientious objection, and the need for respecting the "rules of humanity" during wartime.

First to speak, although out of turn, was Cardinal Ottaviani, who rose slowly from his seat and walked stiffly up to the podium. He was eighty years old now, nearly blind, and the many confrontations of the past few years had clearly taken a toll.

He began: "In my opinion this schema suffers from a number of defects." The delegates braced themselves for another classic Ottaviani diatribe – but they were soon to be mistaken. "For example," he said, "there was no mention of 'the tools of justice and charity needed to overcome wars' such as civic and religious education, an increased use of arbitration, and more respect for the decisions of such international bodies as the International Court of Justice at the Hague and the United Nations."

Ottaviani suddenly had the assembly's rapt attention. "War must not be understood too narrowly or conventionally in the sense of strictly military warfare. The concept should be broadened to include armed revolution, guerrilla activities, and acts of sabotage and terrorism such as those used by communists to bring about the subjugation of other countries."

In an impressively professorial tone, Ottaviani argued that the schema should contain "a sharp reproof of any war waged to impose a particular ideology" and he went on to cite a famous passage from Thomas Aquinas' *Government of Rulers* to the effect that when people see their own government inviting ruin by an aggressive war, they can and must overthrow that government by just means. "The sacred right of rebellion!" Ottaviani thundered, pounding his fist on the podium.

In conclusion, he softened his tone: "War would only be a memory if the words of Pope Paul spoken at the United Nations were fixed forever in the hearts of rulers and people alike."

In this fervid burst of oratory, Cardinal Ottaviani was perhaps carried away by the thought that this might be one of his last appearances before the Council. His eloquence, and in particular his accolade for his frequent theological foe, Pope Paul, was greeted with sincere applause. He descended from the microphone and took his seat, emotionally spent.

<hr />

On October 7th, the Council moved on to debate the Decree on Missionary Activity, which recognized that the role of missionaries throughout the world was in a state of crisis. There were practical issues to be addressed: the drying up of vocations (not only to the missionary field); the unwillingness of some countries to admit missionaries; and the time-consuming burden of fundraising to name a few. Broader questions were also raised in the document. Were missions still relevant in light of the Church's increased emphasis on freedom of conscience and the "elements of truth" to be found in all religions? Why disturb people in their beliefs if they could achieve salvation without the Gospel? Should more efforts be directed toward improving a people's lot economically and socially rather than concentrating strictly on evangelization?

However, before any speakers had a chance to begin debate on the schema, the Council proceedings were unexpectedly halted.

In recent days the Italian press had been publishing sensational reports about the rising number of requests being submitted to the Holy Office from priests desiring to be released from their vow of celibacy. One news outlet, quoting "an anonymous Latin American prelate," stated that there were as many as 10,000 such requests pending and that the issue would be up for discussion during the Fourth Session of Vatican Council II.

Although it was rumored that several Latin American bishops did intend to bring the matter before the Council, no schema for discussion had been prepared or approved in advance.

Alarmed at the prospect of a tumultuous, and likely public, airing of the highly sensitive celibacy question, Eugène Cardinal Tisserant, on behalf of his Curial colleagues, requested an urgent audience with Pope Paul in which he asked the pontiff to act immediately to prevent this discussion from reaching the Council floor. His plea was successful, resulting in the following letter read the next day by Cardinal Tisserant to the assemblage:

> We [Pope Paul] have learned that certain Council Fathers intend to discuss the issue of ecclesiastical celibacy in the Council. Therefore, without infringing in any way on the right of the Fathers to express themselves, we make known to you our personal opinion that this is not the opportunity to have a public discussion of this topic, which demands so much prudence and is so important. We not only intend to maintain this ancient, holy, and providential law of celibacy but also to reinforce its observance, calling on all priests to recognize anew the causes and reasons why this law must be considered most appropriate today, especially today, in helping priests to consecrate all their love completely and generously to Christ in the service of the Church.

Pope Paul's letter unequivocally ruled out any possibility that the issue of priestly celibacy would be discussed during Vatican Council II.

Severely disappointed, Dutch Bishop Gerardus Koop rose to speak. What he wanted, and presumably so did others who intended to discuss the issue, was not an abolition of the law of celibacy but rather a modification of the existing code that would permit a married clergy to operate alongside a celibate clergy. This would be especially relevant in areas like Latin America, he argued, where the pastoral needs were so immense and the possibility of meeting them with the existing numbers of priests almost nil.

John Cardinal Heenan of England then rose to speak, not directly on the issue of celibacy but rather on something that he considered even more crucial, the generally taboo subject of "fallen" priests who had "acted immorally." Heenan contended that it was important for the Council to say something definitive about a priest's responsibility to report such behavior by another priest. "When a wretched man has made a shipwreck of his priestly life," he said, "his fellow priests, unhappily, rarely speak up in time. In this matter they are inclined to behave like schoolboys. At all costs they do not want to be regarded as sneaks or informers so they remain silent while a brother priest rushes to his ruin."

Unfortunately, given the sternness of the pope's letter, Heenan's remarkably prescient admonition was dismissed to no avail.

Few Council documents were followed with as much scrutiny as the renamed Declaration on the Jews, later to be incorporated into a more broadly constructed Declaration on Relations with Non-Christian Religions (including Hindus, Buddhists, Moslems, as well as Jews). However, it was on the Jewish portion that attention was almost exclusively focused, largely because of the intense interest shown by certain Jewish groups, most notably the American Jewish Committee. Ironically, the Council found itself in the rather anomalous position of dealing with a subject that seemed at times to be of greater moment to Jews than to the Christians for whom its statement was primarily intended.

In essence, the Declaration on the Jews tried to do three things: reaffirm the close historic ties that bound Jews and Christians together; eliminate the age-old charge of "deicide" (literally the crime of killing God in the person of Jesus Christ); and extinguish once and for all the flames of Christian anti-Semitism.

The history of this document had been stormy. It originated as an idea of Pope John in 1960. However, bowing to pressure from Arab states as well as ultra-conservative voices within the Curia, it was not brought up during the First Session.

When Pope Paul placed it on the proposed agendas for the Second and Third Sessions, conservative forces within the Curia coalesced once again, claiming that because of a "lack of time" to adequately research such an important matter, any debate on the Jewish question would have to be postponed. Pope Paul, unfortunately, yielded in both instances.

Paul was therefore adamant that the Declaration on the Jews would be debated and successfully voted upon during the Fourth Session, and he personally intervened in the preparation of the schema to be presented to the Council Fathers. As a result of his efforts, it was assumed that the document would easily win a majority when it was scheduled for a vote on October 14th, the only question being the extent of discontent over the omission of the word "deicide." An alarming and anonymous letter had been sent to Pope Paul threatening to blow up St. Peter's Basilica if the Jewish declaration was brought to a vote. Unfazed, Pope Paul mandated that the balloting commence immediately, although security throughout the basilica was heightened considerably. Fortunately, except for a resounding crash when some workmen's scaffolding collapsed, the voting proceeded without incident. The result: 1,763 for the motion approving the Declaration on the Jews versus 250 against. This ensured that it would be officially promulgated by the close of the Council, albeit buried within the broader Declaration on Relations with Non-Christian Religions.

The numerically far superior and finally emboldened progressive majority had begun exerting its theological muscle. By the end of October, four additional schema were debated and successfully approved in quick succession:

- Decree on the Pastoral Office of Bishops, which clarified the roles and responsibilities of bishops within their respective dioceses;
- Decree on the Renewal of Religious Life, which encouraged religious men and women to return

to the core values and missions of their religious orders;

- Decree on the Formation of Priests, which called for a more comprehensive and contemporary approach to the education of future priests; and,
- Declaration on Christian Education, which emphasized the importance of education in the faith, both in schools and in the family.

The momentum continued with debates and subsequent approvals for two additional documents on November 18th:

- Decree on the Apostolate of the Laity, which called for an increased role of lay persons in religious services; and,
- The all-important Constitution on Divine Revelation, which reaffirmed that divine revelation comes from both sacred scripture and the descendants of the apostles (bishops and clergy).

This left only four schema to be debated during the remaining weeks of the Fourth Session: the Declaration on Religious Freedom; the Decree on Missionary Activity; the Declaration on Relations with Non-Christian Religions (incorporating the Declaration on the Jews); and the many contentious components of Schema 13 involving the Church's role in contemporary society.

Gone was the mood of uncertainty and pessimism that had prevailed throughout the Third Session. It was now clear that tangible, arguably historic, progress was being made and that the end of the Council's work was in sight.

———◆———

Father Murphy met Robert and Anna Ferraro upon their arrival at Rome's Fiumicino Airport. They were a young American couple, in their early thirties, who had been corresponding with him for months and thereafter with Luciana and the good sisters of Villa Nazareth. After years of trying to conceive on their own, their dream of finally having a child through adoption was close, their anticipation almost unbearable. They would soon meet Isabella, a beautiful four-year-old girl who had been raised at Villa Nazareth since being abandoned shortly after her birth.

The taxi ride from the airport seemed excruciatingly long for the Ferraros. Murphy occasionally interjected mild conversation, but they were too excited to respond. As they pulled up to the orphanage, its large, aging wooden front door creaked open and three nuns emerged with a small, nervous child enfolded within their habits. Luciana stood respectfully a few yards behind them and off to the side.

Unrestrained joy overtook the Ferraros as they exited the taxi and walked excitedly toward the group. However, Isabella suddenly broke free and ran up to hug them. It was an incredible, heartwarming moment. All, including Murphy, shed tears.

The Mother Superior motioned everyone inside to a small conference room. Luciana handed the Ferraros a file with all of the necessary documentation, congratulated them both, then turned and lovingly embraced Isabella, tears streaming down her face. Murphy, similarly moved, did the same. Then they both walked out together to Luciana's waiting car.

"We have finally begun," she said, still clearly emotional as they climbed into the back seat.

"*You* have just begun," Murphy quietly interjected. She looked at him uncertainly. He continued, almost in a whisper. "Luciana, I am proud to have helped you at the start of this wonderful endeavor – reaching out to my friends back in the States, following up with prospective families, and forwarding the most promising of them directly to you." He looked out the window toward the orphanage. "And we have just witnessed the first fruit of those labors." He turned to her and grasped her hands in his. "However, my time in Rome is coming to an end and, truly, you can now continue on without me." She began to interrupt but he stopped her. "Luciana, it is my wish."

She began crying intensely. When she finally composed herself, a halting "Yes…I understand," was all she could muster. Then, after a few moments she said, "But first let us celebrate." She turned to her driver, "Harry's Bar, please."

On Saturday, December 4th, four days before the Fourth Session – and Vatican Council II itself – would come to an end, Pope Paul took part with all of the non-Catholic observer delegates and a vast majority of the Council Fathers in an unprecedented interdenominational "Liturgy of the Word" in the Basilica of St. Paul Outside the Walls. Not by coincidence, it was where Pope John had first announced his intention to summon an Ecumenical Council over six years earlier. The service consisted of prayers, psalms, and lessons from Scripture derived from Catholic, Protestant, and Orthodox traditions. The hymn "Now Thank We All Our God," written by the seventeenth-century Lutheran composer Johann Crüger, followed the readings.

In the course of his moving sermon, the pope declared to the observer delegates, "We would like to have you with us always." The Council, he said, had shown that reunion could eventually be achieved, "slowly, gradually, loyally, and generously."

As one of the Protestant observers commented later, "The service was one of the most impressive moments of the whole Council."

Unfortunately, a number of conservative cardinals and bishops refused to attend. Professing to be scandalized, they sent a message to the pope the following morning, expressing their amazement at the encouragement he had given to what they had been taught to believe was a *communicatio in sacris* with heretics. The pope, incredulous, did not dignify their message with a response.

———————— ◆ ————————

On Monday, December 6, 1965, Pope Paul stunned the assemblage by announcing that the Congregation of the Holy Office, headed by Cardinal Ottaviani, was to be completely reconstituted. First, he said, its present name, recalling undesirable memories of the "Holy Inquisition," was to be dropped in favor of the less alarming "Congregation for the Doctrine of the Faith." He then stipulated that the new congregation would be more concerned with promoting theological research and investigation rather than heresy hunting. While the Index of Prohibited Books would remain under its jurisdiction, there would be an important change with respect to authors who might be denounced for heterodoxy. Instead of being condemned in silence and very often without being able to offer any defense, such persons were henceforth to have the right to defend themselves according to accepted and published norms. Furthermore, no action would be taken against anyone without first informing their local bishop.

There were strong rumors that, in conjunction with these actions, the pope had requested Cardinal Ottaviani's resignation on his desk. This was rebutted by members of the Holy Office staff, but when the Vatican newspaper, *L'Osservatore Romano,* failed to publish an official denial, most saw it as a sign that the rumors were likely true.

During the final week of the Fourth Session, the pope managed to visit with an extraordinary number of people to express his personal gratitude for their efforts throughout the Council. He chose the beautiful Sala Clementina in the Apostolic Palace for the audiences. Built during the pontificate of Pope Clement VIII in 1600, its magnificent frescoes, gilded moldings, ornate stucco decorations, and coffered ceiling provided an awe-inspiring backdrop. Not only bishops and cardinals involved with the Conciliar deliberations were invited to these events but also many of those in supporting roles such as Council *periti*, and even handymen and chauffeurs.

However, a special audience with the pope was reserved for Father Francis Xavier Murphy, with only Monsignor Benelli and Father Macchi in attendance.

Upon entering, Father Murphy kneeled and kissed the papal ring. When he rose, Pope Paul smiled and said, "Great is your faithfulness. As is your courage. Please know the depth of my gratitude for your very special contribution to the success of the Council." And with that, he made the sign of the cross, reciting from the Book of Numbers: "The Lord bless you and keep you; the Lord make His face to shine upon you and be gracious to you; the Lord lift up His countenance upon you and give you peace."

Murphy, moved to tears, bowed, looked to Benelli and Macchi who were in tears themselves, then solemnly took his leave.

On December 7th, the final four documents of the Fourth Session were voted on and approved:

- Declaration on Religious Freedom, which emphasized the rights of individuals to practice their religion according to their own conscience, and for governments to respect the religious liberty of their citizens;
- Decree on Missionary Activity, which clarified the role of missionaries in proclaiming the mission of the Church throughout the world;
- Declaration on Relations with Non-Christian Religions, including its modified Declaration on the Jews, which called for increasing dialogue and tolerance for all faiths; and,
- Pastoral Constitution on the Church in the Modern World, which took a first step toward addressing the Church's involvement in contemporary societal issues.

The latter included many aspects of the hugely controversial Schema 13, with the notable exception of the Catholic Church's official position on birth control. Pope Paul notified the Council Fathers that he would address that issue separately in a forthcoming encyclical.

THE MOLE OF VATICAN COUNCIL II

As soon as these final declarations of Vatican Council II were officially promulgated, Cardinal Siri and Cardinal Ottaviani walked out of St. Peter's Basilica together, arm-in-arm, with Siri supporting his elderly colleague. As they crossed the vast piazza, Siri sensed his friend's emotion.

"The proclamations are not definitive; they will never bind us," Siri declared.

They walked a few more steps, then Cardinal Ottaviani stopped and turned, looking back at the magnificent basilica that had consumed so much of his energy, of his life, over the past few years. "We must accept the things we cannot change," he counseled Siri, ironically paraphrasing a Lutheran theologian, Reinhold Niebuhr. "My world has passed, but yours is yet unfolding. Be prudent, my friend."

He turned back around and they continued walking, slowly, as the late afternoon shadows enveloped them.

The Closing Ceremony took place the following day, December 8, 1965, in the open air of St. Peter's Square. The 2,500 delegates gathered in their regular Council seats inside the basilica, many of them wearing the gold rings that Pope Paul had given them to commemorate the work of the Council. They then processed outside to temporary banks of bleachers set up adjacent to a raised papal throne and altar. Once they were seated, Pope Paul appeared, again wearing a bishop's mitre to emphasize his collegiality with his brethren.

After a solemn Mass, the pope read a series of "conciliar messages to the world," intended to embrace all categories of the human family whom the Council had tried to reach, including rulers, scholars, artists, women, workingmen, youth, the poor and the sick, among others. Archbishop Felici then read a document proclaiming the official closing of Vatican Council II, after which five bishops representing five continents chanted ancient invocations that had been used to close Ecumenical Councils since that of Chalcedon in the year 451.

Once they finished, Pope Paul rose and dismissed the assembly with a simple, yet profound blessing, "*Ite in pace* – Go in peace."

***

Father Murphy, moved by the remarkable ceremony he had just witnessed, and reflecting on his own crucial role in this historic event for the Catholic Church, walked pensively back to his apartment at the Accademia Alfonsiana and began writing what would be his final article for *The New Yorker*:

> Vatican Council II reached its formal close here today, though it may be said that its real work is just beginning. The idea of holding the Council came to Pope John XXIII on January 20, 1959.

("The first to be surprised by this proposal of mine was myself," the pope wrote in his journal.) It was convened on October 11, 1962, and after Pope John's death in 1963 was reconvened by Pope Paul VI....

In its four annual sessions, the Council has promulgated more than a dozen decrees. According to the official record keepers, some twenty-five hundred Council Fathers cast a total of one million, two hundred thousand individual ballots on the various texts put to them, and they wrote some six thousand speeches, of which fourteen hundred were delivered on the Council floor. It was not the longest Council in the history of the Church – the Council of Trent holds that record of eighteen years – but it was beyond question the most important religious event this century has yet seen....

After a detailed summation of the many challenges faced, and mostly overcome, during the Fourth Session, Murphy concluded with caution toward the future:

Some answers have been provided by Vatican II, but more questions have been raised. As one delegate was overheard to remark at the Council's end, "Far less has been accomplished than has been made possible. More frontiers have been opened than occupied." Nonetheless, Pope John's vision of *aggiornamento* for the Catholic Church has indeed been fulfilled.[9]

———— ◆ ————

Murphy had written throughout the night, in contemplative fits and starts, and it was suddenly early dawn. Sunlight, partially obscured by intermittent clouds, streamed hopefully into his apartment. He walked over to his window, opened it wide, and inhaled the fresh, invigorating air.

---

[9] "Letter from Vatican City," *The New Yorker*, December 25, 1965

Epilogue

———◆———

Soon after the conclusion of Vatican Council II,
Father Francis Xavier Murphy returned to the
United States and assumed teaching posts at Princeton and Johns Hopkins Universities, was appointed Rector of Holy Redeemer College in Washington, DC, and
then moved to St. Mary's Parish in Annapolis, Maryland,
where he served as a parish priest and continued with his
prodigious writing career. Over the course of his lifetime,
he wrote more than thirty books and penned hundreds
of articles on topics ranging from the early history of
Christianity to contemporary issues affecting the Catholic
Church – in addition to the pivotal articles he wrote for
The New Yorker throughout the Second Vatican Council.
He is widely considered to have been one of the most
important religious writers of his day and was awarded a
Lifetime Achievement Award by the National Arts Club in
New York in 1998. He died in 2002.

On July 5, 2013, Pope Francis declared Pope John XXIII a saint, bypassing many of the traditional benchmarks for consideration of sainthood, due in large measure to his calling forth of Vatican Council II. In a similar fashion, he canonized Pope Paul VI on October 14, 2018, emphasizing his leadership toward the successful completion of the Council. Their immediate successors, Pope John Paul I and Pope John Paul II, chose their pontifical names to underscore their support for the ideals espoused by Vatican Council II.

Alfredo Cardinal Ottaviani resigned from his Vatican duties shortly after the conclusion of the Second Vatican Council. In 1970, Pope Paul restricted voting in papal enclaves to cardinals under the age of eighty. Cardinal Ottaviani took this as a personal affront, given his sudden ineligibility, calling the pope's move "an act committed in contempt of a tradition that is centuries old." He died in 1979.

Giovanni Benelli was appointed by Pope Paul to be his Deputy Secretary of State in 1967 and he was elevated by Paul to the rank of cardinal in 1977. He served as the Archbishop of Florence from 1977 until his death in 1982.

Pasquale Macchi continued to serve as Pope Paul's personal secretary throughout his papacy, after which he held a variety of Vatican posts. He was appointed Archbishop of Loreto, Italy, by Pope John Paul II in 1989, a position he retained until 1996. He passed away in 2006.

Pietro Parente continued to work in the renamed Congregation for the Doctrine of the Faith (formerly Holy Office, Inquisition) until he was elevated to the cardinalate by Pope Paul in 1967. He served as the Cardinal-Priest of San Lorenzo in Lucina, Italy, until his death in 1986.

Giuseppe Siri served as the Archbishop of Genoa from 1946-1987, being elevated to the cardinalate in 1953 by Pope Pius XII. He died in 1989, having never achieved his ambition of sitting on the Throne of St. Peter.

Loris Capovilla served as Pope John XXIII's personal secretary from 1958-1963. He was appointed Archbishop of Chieti-Vasto, Italy, by Pope Paul in 1967 and elevated by Pope Francis to the cardinalate in 2014, serving at the Basilica of Santa Maria in Trastavere in Rome until his passing in 2016.

Cristina and Luciana are fictional characters considered essential by the author to the overall storyline.

Villa Nazareth, founded by then-Monsignor Domenico Tardini in 1946, continues to this day as a home for disadvantaged but talented youth under the auspices of the Vatican Secretariat of State.

Vatican Council II's legacy has been the subject of ongoing interpretation and debate within the Catholic

Church since its closing in 1965. Most Catholics around the world have embraced the changes and reforms brought about by the Council, the most visible of which include the celebration of Mass in their local language instead of Latin and the increased participation of laity in the mission of the Church. However, there remain staunch critics of the Council, both inside and outside the Church, who contend, among other concerns, that the Council summarily cast aside centuries of established Church protocols and traditions to address short-term societal issues.

Without question, Vatican Council II marked one of the most significant turning points in the two-millennia history of the Roman Catholic Church, and its impact will continue to shape the Church's engagement in the modern world for years to come. However, its legacy cannot be completely understood without knowing the remarkable story of "Xavier Rynne," the Redemptorist priest Father Francis X. Murphy.

About the Author

Prior to writing *The Mole of Vatican Council II*, Richard Zmuda previously co-authored a pair of non-fiction books for cancer survivors (*I Flunked My Mammogram: What Every Woman Needs To Know About Breast Cancer; I Flunked My PSA: What You Need To Know About Prostate Cancer Now!*). For twenty years he served as the editor of the Johns Hopkins Breast Center's online patient educational magazine, *Artemis*. After the passing of his first wife from breast cancer, he wrote an anecdotal autobiography, *A Father's Notes,* excerpts from which were published in

Chicken Soup for the Soul and *Chicken Soup for the Single Parent's Soul.*

Richard has also written a play for middle-school and high-school students, *Apollo 11: Original Adaptation for the Stage,* to inspire a new generation of space scientists, and he published a children's book in 2016 titled, *'Cuz That's Just My Way,* that offers a beautiful lesson on tolerance.

He recently retired after teaching literature for twenty-three years at the high school level in Maryland and is currently working on a collection of short stories inspired by the artwork of Winslow Homer. He is enjoying life in Annapolis, Maryland, with his wife Kim and their new black lab Jack!

Acknowledgments

Well in advance of my first trip to Rome to research this book, I made an appointment with a high-ranking bishop to review files that had been kept on Father Murphy. Upon my arrival, I was instead greeted by an elderly Spanish priest who apologized profusely that the bishop "had gone for a long walk" and was not available to meet with me. He then handed me a file from the bishop containing only Father Murphy's *curriculum vitae*. "There must be some mistake," he said, confused. "We have many files on Father Murphy." He left, only to return a few minutes later with boxes of information. I furiously plowed through the trove of documents, gleaning incredible details on how the Vatican had tracked Father Murphy's activities throughout his tenure in Rome but also including alarmingly personal information on him as well. I'll never know what wrath that wonderfully naive priest faced upon the bishop's return, but those insights were crucial to the narrative of this book.

I am similarly grateful to other individuals, both in Rome and the United States, who gave me access to other files that had been kept on Father Murphy, almost certainly without his knowledge. They know who they are.

Finally, special thanks to Greg Pierce of ACTA Publications for his meticulous editing skills and to Kimberly Taft for her keen literary insights as this storyline unfolded.

APPENDIX

Ecumenical Councils of the Roman Catholic Church

Ecumenical Council: a worldwide convocation of church leaders and theological experts convened to discuss crucial matters of doctrine and practice. In the 2,000-year history of the Roman Catholic Church there have only been twenty-one Ecumenical Councils.
(Source: *The Catholic Encyclopedia*)

I. FIRST COUNCIL OF NICAEA
Year: 325
The Council of Nicaea lasted two months and twelve days. Three hundred and eighteen bishops were present. Hosius, Bishop of Cordova, assisted as legate of Pope Sylvester. The Emperor Constantine was also present. This Council was responsible for the Nicene Creed and fixing of the date for keeping Easter.

II. FIRST COUNCIL OF CONSTANTINOPLE
Year: 381

The First General Council of Constantinople, under Pope Damasus and the Emperor Theodosius I, was attended by 150 bishops. It was directed against the followers of Macedonius, who impugned the Divinity of the Holy Ghost. To the above-mentioned Nicene Creed it added the clauses referring to the Holy Ghost (*qui simul adoratur*) and all that follows to the end.

III. COUNCIL OF EPHESUS
Year: 431

The Council of Ephesus, attended by more than 200 bishops, was presided over by St. Cyril of Alexandria, representing Pope Celestine I. It defined the true personal unity of Christ, declared Mary the Mother of God (*theotokos*), and renewed the condemnation of Pelagius.

IV. COUNCIL OF CHALCEDON
Year: 451

The Council of Chalcedon, attended by 150 bishops under Pope Leo the Great and the Emperor Marcian, defined the two natures (divine and human) in Christ.

V. SECOND COUNCIL OF CONSTANTINOPLE
Year: 553

The Second General Council of Constantinople, with 165 bishops under Pope Vigilius and Emperor

Justinian I, condemned the errors of Origen and certain other writings. It further confirmed the first four General Councils, especially that of Chalcedon, whose authority was being contested by some heretics.

VI. THIRD COUNCIL OF CONSTANTINOPLE
Years: 680-681

The Third General Council of Constantinople, under Pope Agatho and the Emperor Constantine Pogonatus, was attended by the Patriarchs of Constantinople and of Antioch, 174 bishops, and the emperor. It put an end to Monothelitism by defining two wills in Christ, the divine and the human, as two distinct principles of operation.

VII. SECOND COUNCIL OF NICAEA
Year: 787

The Second Council of Nicaea was convoked by Emperor Constantine VI and his mother Irene, under Pope Adrian I, and was presided over by the legates of Pope Adrian. It regulated the veneration of holy images. Between 300 and 367 bishops attended.

VIII. FOURTH COUNCIL OF CONSTANTINOPLE
Year: 869

The Fourth General Council of Constantinople, under Pope Adrian II and Emperor Basil, included 102 bishops, three papal legates, and four patriarchs. It consigned to the flames the Acts of an irregular council (*conciliabulum*) that had been brought together by Photius against Pope Nicholas and Ignatius, the legitimate Patriarch of Constantinople. It condemned Photius, who had unlawfully seized the patriarchal dignity. The "Photian Schism," however, triumphed in the Greek Church, and no other General Council has since taken place in the East.

IX. FIRST LATERAN COUNCIL
Year: 1123

The First Lateran Council, the first Council held in Rome, met under Pope Callistus II. About 900 bishops and abbots attended. It abolished the right claimed by lay princes of investiture with ring and crosier to ecclesiastical benefices and dealt with church discipline and the recovery of the Holy Land from the so-named "infidels."

X. SECOND LATERAN COUNCIL
Year: 1139

The Second Lateran Council was held in Rome under Pope Innocent II, with an attendance of about 1,000 prelates and the Emperor Conrad. Its object was to put an end to the errors of Arnold of Brescia.

XI. THIRD LATERAN COUNCIL
Year: 1179

The Third Lateran Council in Rome took place under

Pope Alexander III, Frederick I being emperor. There were 302 bishops present. It condemned the Albigenses and Waldenses and issued numerous decrees for the reformation of morals.

XII. FOURTH LATERAN COUNCIL
Year: 1215

The Fourth Lateran Council in Rome was held under Innocent III. Present were the Patriarchs of Constantinople and Jerusalem, seventy-one archbishops, 412 bishops, 800 abbots, the Primate of the Maronites, and St. Dominic. It issued an enlarged creed against the Albigenses (*Firmiter credimus*), condemned the Trinitarian errors of Abbot Joachim, and published seventy reformatory decrees. This was the most important Council of the Middle Ages and was the culminating point of ecclesiastical life and papal power in the Middle Ages.

XIII. FIRST COUNCIL OF LYONS
Year: 1245

The First General Council of Lyons in France was presided over by Innocent IV and included the Patriarchs of Constantinople, Antioch, and Aquileia (Venice); 140 bishops; Baldwin II, Emperor of the East; and St. Louis, King of France. It excommunicated and deposed Emperor Frederick II and directed a new crusade, under the command of St. Louis, against the Saracens and Mongols.

XIV. SECOND COUNCIL OF LYONS
Year: 1274

The Second General Council of Lyons was held by Pope Gregory X, the Patriarchs of Antioch and Constantinople, and included fifteen cardinals, 500 bishops, and more than 1,000 other dignitaries. It effected a temporary reunion of the Greek Church with Rome. The word *filioque* was added to the crest of Constantinople and means were sought for recovering Palestine from the Turks. It also laid down the rules for papal elections.

XV. COUNCIL OF VIENNE
Years: 1311-1313

The Council of Vienne was held in that town in France by order of Clement V, the first of the Avignon popes. The Patriarchs of Antioch and Alexandria, 300 bishops (114 according to some authorities), and three kings – Philip IV of France, Edward II of England, and James II of Aragon – were present. The Council dealt with the crimes and errors imputed to the Knights Templar, the Fraticelli, the Beghards, and the Beguines, initiating projects of a new crusade, the reformation of the clergy, and the teaching of Oriental languages in the universities.

XVI. COUNCIL OF CONSTANCE
Years: 1414-1418

The Council of Constance was held during the great Schism of the West, with the object of ending the divisions in the Church. It became legitimate only when Gregory XII formally convoked it. Owing to this circumstance, it succeeded in putting an end to the schism by the election of Pope Martin V, which the rogue Council of Pisa (1403) had failed to accomplish on account of its illegality. The new and rightful pope confirmed the former decrees of the synod against Wyclif and Hus. This Council is thus ecumenical only in its last sessions (42-45 inclusive) and with respect to the decrees of earlier sessions approved by Martin V.

XVII. COUNCIL OF BASLE/FERRARA/FLORENCE

Years: 1431-1439

The Council of Basle met first in that town in Italy, Eugene IV being pope and Sigismund the emperor of the Holy Roman Empire. Its object was the religious pacification of Bohemia. Quarrels with the pope having arisen, the Council was transferred first to the Italian towns of Ferrara (1438) and then Florence (1439), where a short-lived union with the Greek Church was effected, the Greeks accepting the Council's definition of controverted points. The Council of Basle was only ecumenical until the end of the twenty-fifth session, and of its decrees Eugene IV approved only such as dealt with the extirpation of heresy, the peace of Christendom, and the reform of the Church, and which at the same time did not derogate from the rights of the Holy See of Rome.

XVIII. FIFTH LATERAN COUNCIL
Years: 1512-1517

The Fifth Lateran Council in Rome met under Popes Julius II and Leo X, the emperor being Maximilian I. Fifteen cardinals and about eighty archbishops and bishops took part. Its decrees were chiefly disciplinary. A new crusade against the Turks was also planned, but came to naught owing to the religious upheaval in Germany caused by Martin Luther.

XIX. COUNCIL OF TRENT
Years: 1545-1563

The Council of Trent lasted eighteen years under five popes: Paul III, Julius III, Marcellus II, Paul IV, and Pius IV, and under the emperors Charles V and Ferdinand. There were present five cardinal legates of the Holy See, three patriarchs, thirty-three archbishops, 235 bishops, seven abbots, seven superior generals of monastic orders, and 160 doctors of divinity. It was convoked to examine and condemn the errors promulgated by Martin Luther and other Reformers, and to reform the discipline of the Church. Of all the Councils of the Church, it lasted longest, issued the largest number of dogmatic and reformatory decrees, and arguably produced the most beneficial results.

XX. FIRST VATICAN COUNCIL
Years: 1869-1870

Vatican Council I was summoned by Pius IX and met in Rome. Present were six archbishop-princes, forty-nine cardinals, eleven patriarchs, 680 archbishops and bishops, twenty-eight abbots, and twenty-nine superior generals of religious orders. Besides important canons relating to the faith and the constitution of the Church, the Council decreed the infallibility of the pope when speaking *ex cathedra*, i.e., when as shepherd and teacher of all Christians, he defines a doctrine concerning faith or morals to be held by the whole Church.

XXI. SECOND VATICAN COUNCIL
Years: 1962-1965

Vatican Council II was called by Pope John XXIII almost 100 years after Vatican I and 400 years after the Council of Trent. It was brought to completion by Pope Paul VI. Present were some 2,500 voting cardinals and bishops, in addition to observer-delegates from other Christian denominations and non-Christian faiths. Despite considerable resistance from conservative cardinals in the Curia, the Council successfully promulgated more than a dozen decrees intended to bring the Catholic Church up-to-date in the modern world.

Other Books on Post-Vatican II Catholicism

The Cardinal's Assassin, Under Pain of
Mortal Sin, Master of Ceremonies
trilogy of ecclesial novels by Donald Cozzens

Church Chicago Style
by William Droel

Ed Marciniak's City and Church
by Charles Shanabruch

God Shed His Grace on Thee
by Carol DeChant

Invitation to Catholicism
by Alice Camille

The Mass Is Never Ended and *The World As It Should* Be
by Gregory Pierce

Silent Schism and *All Things to All People*
by Brother Louis DeThomasis

Available from booksellers and ACTA Publications
www.actapublications.com 800-397-2282